Mobile
Art

Mobile ART

Make your home a magical
place with these 35 beautiful
hanging decorations

CLARE YOUNGS

CICO BOOKS

LONDON NEW YORK

I would like to dedicate this book to Claire Richardson who was an amazingly talented photographer, a joy to work with, and a dear friend.

Published in 2015 by CICO Books
An imprint of Ryland Peters & Small Ltd

20–21 Jockey's Fields
London WC1R 4BW

341 E 116th St
New York, NY 10029

www.rylandpeters.com

10 9 8 7 6 5 4 3 2 1

A CIP catalog record for this book is available from the Library of Congress and the British Library.

ISBN: 978-1-78249-209-2

Printed in China

Editor: Anna Southgate
Designer: Elizabeth Healey
Photographer: James Gardiner
Illustrator: Ian Youngs
Stylist: Clare Youngs

In-house editor: Anna Galkina
In-house designer: Fahema Khanam
Art director: Sally Powell
Head of production: Patricia Harrington
Publishing manager: Penny Craig
Publisher: Cindy Richards

CONTENTS

INTRODUCTION

Suspend an object from a piece of string, hang it from the ceiling, and you have a mobile. It can be as simple as that. With a little more time, you can carefully balance wires and thread to create a decoration that changes constantly with the movement of air in a room. Either way, a mobile is an endless source of fascination and wonder.

There are mobiles to suit all ages and all tastes. A baby staring up from the crib will focus on a shifting pattern of color and shape. A child will delight as a herd of sleepy elephants twists and dances in the air. A geometric himmeli mobile will create a focal point of contemporary sophistication in your living room.

Since the artist Alexander Calder first introduced the mobile in the 1930s, they have become increasingly popular in the world of art and interior decoration. When my children were very little I looked around for mobiles to decorate their bedrooms. Not being able to find the perfect ones, I set about making them myself. I soon discovered that not only do they look totally brilliant, but they are also great fun to make!

Better still, this is a great craft to involve the kids in—they rarely need encouragement to play with paper and glue. Simple objects foraged on a woodland walk or even collected from the back yard can provide materials, with stunning results. Objects that usually get discarded by the back door, take on a new beauty when they are suspended from thread, creating ever-changing shadows as they gently move in the air. Whether you use fallen leaves, seedpods, shells, or pebbles, the decoration will be a wonderful reminder of your adventures together.

Making mobiles can be light on your pocket—you probably have many of the basic materials on hand at home: scraps of paper, card stock (card), fabric, sewing thread, embroidery floss (thread), and found objects. You will learn different methods of construction so that you can create your own unique decorations for your home or to give as presents to friends and family. Not only will they appreciate your efforts, but they will be amazed at the simple, sculptural beauty of your work.

GEOMETRIC FUN

Folded Chevrons

This striking mobile is extremely economical because it is constructed from white printer paper. I like the stylish simplicity of white for this project, but you could use any paper you like. Bright primary colors or pretty Japanese papers would give equally successful results.

YOU WILL NEED

- *Printer paper*
- *Pencil*
- *Ruler*
- *Scissors*
- *Florist's bare stem wire*
- *Wire cutters*
- *Pliers*
- *Needle and nylon thread*

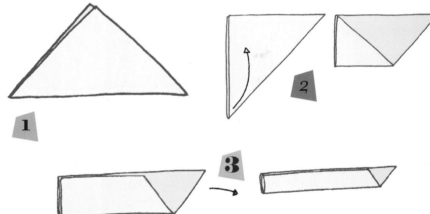

1 Take a sheet of printer paper and draw a square measuring 8¼ x 8¼ in. (21 x 21 cm). Cut out the square and fold it in half to make a triangle. Open out the square and re-fold along the crease line, but in the opposite direction so that you have neither a valley nor a mountain fold, but a universal fold (one that can fold either way).

2 Position the triangle as shown, and bring the bottom corner up to meet the top corner. Press along the crease.

3 Now bring the bottom edge up to meet the top edge and press along the crease. Repeat one more time. You will have divided the square into eight parts.

4 Unfold the paper, to return to the triangle shape you made in Step 1. Remake each of the new folds—this time in the opposite direction—to make a universal fold each time.

5 Now open up the paper square completely. Holding the square gently on either side of the center fold, manipulate the longest fold to make a mountain fold.

6 Manipulate the next fold to make a valley fold, and so on as you move on to each subsequent fold. As you go, the square will concertina to make a chevron shape.

7 Follow Steps 1 to 6 to make three chevrons from 8¼ x 8¼ in. (21 x 21 cm) paper squares and two from paper squares measuring 6 x 6 in. (15 x 15 cm).

8 Cut three lengths of florist's bare stem wire, one measuring 14½ in. (37 cm) and two measuring 6¼ in. (16 cm). Use pliers to bend the ends of the three wires back on themselves, making a small loop at each end.

9 Thread a needle with a length of nylon thread measuring 13 in. (33 cm) and push it through the top of one of the larger chevrons. Secure with a knot and tie the opposite end to the center of the longest length of wire.

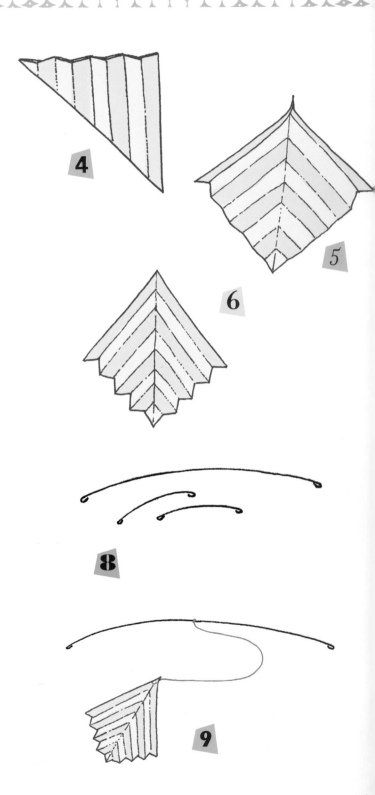

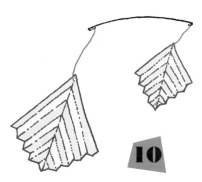

10

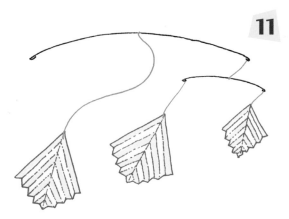

11

10 Thread the remaining chevrons in the same way, each with 6 in. (15 cm) of thread. Attach one large chevron and one small chevron to opposite ends of each of the two remaining lengths of wire. Thread the wire through the loops you made in Step 8, and make sure they hang at slightly different heights.

11 Tie a thread to one of the smaller wires, positioning it roughly at its center, and attach the opposite end of the thread to the loop at one end of the longer wire.

12 Repeat with the second smaller wire, attaching it to the opposite end of the longer wire. Be sure to vary the length of the threads so that the chevrons on one side hang higher or lower than those on the other side.

13 Attach a length of thread to the center of the longer wire, for hanging. You need to address the balance now. Hold the mobile up by the central thread and slide the threads along the smaller wires to the right or left until you reach a point of balance.

HiMMEli

Himmeli sculptures are traditional Finnish decorations made from straws. They have become popular in recent years with the ongoing trend for all things geometric. You can use natural straw, available from craft suppliers, but I have made my project using thin, black drinking straws for a stylish contemporary look. I love the simple clean, graphic lines of this mobile.

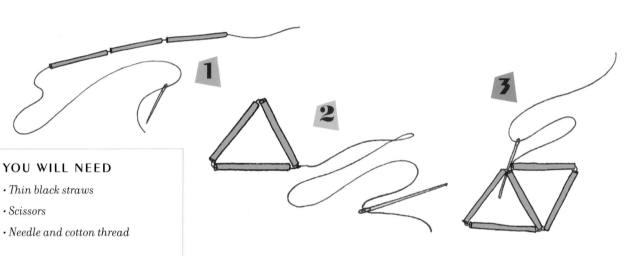

YOU WILL NEED

· *Thin black straws*
· *Scissors*
· *Needle and cotton thread*

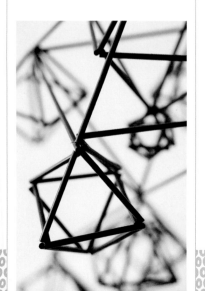

1 My straws measured 5 in. (13 cm) in length. If your straws are longer you can cut them down. You need 12 straws to make the first shape. Start by cutting a long length of cotton and thread it through the needle. Thread three straws on to the cotton, leaving 2 in. (5 cm) of spare thread at the end.

2 Arrange the three straws to make a triangle and tie a knot to secure. Trim off any spare thread.

3 Thread on two more straws and secure with a knot at the top corner of the first triangle.

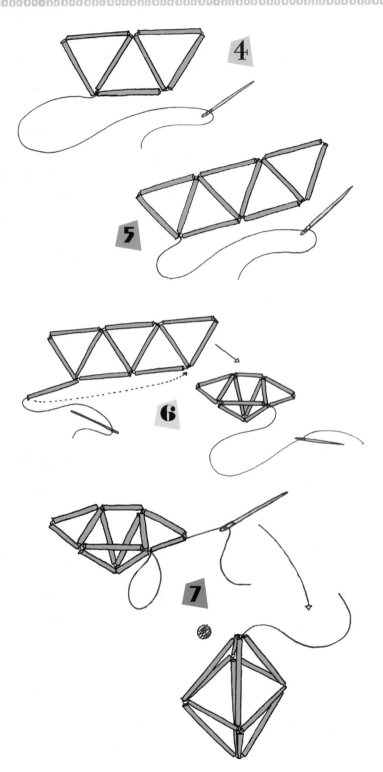

4 Add two more straws and secure them with a knot at the bottom left-hand corner of the first triangle.

5 Continue adding straws in the same way to make a row of triangles using 11 straws.

6 Thread on one more straw and swing it around so that it meets up with the farthest corner in the row of triangles, as shown. Secure with a knot.

7 You will have a 3-D pyramid shape with two triangles attached to two sides of a square base. Thread the needle through the straw that makes up one side of the triangle to the right. Bring the two triangles up to meet together at the top and secure with a knot. This completes one shape.

8 Follow Steps 1 to 7 using different length straws to make a number of shapes in different sizes. I have hung smaller shapes inside—and from the corners of—bigger shapes for my sculpture, but you can make yours as simple or as complex as you like.

9 To produce the mobile shown here you will need the following shapes (measurements given represent straw length):
1 x 5 in. (13 cm)
1 x 2¾ in. (7 cm)
1 x 1⅛ in. (3 cm)

4 x 2 in. (5 cm)

1 x 4 in. (10 cm)

1 x 2⅓ in. (6 cm)

1 x 2½ in. (6.5 cm)

5 x 1¾ in. (4.5 cm)

Hanging within the 5 in. (13 cm) shape, secured at the top with cotton thread, is a 2¾ in. (7 cm) shape. Suspended from the bottom of that is a 1⅛ in. (3 cm) shape. From each corner of the 5 in. (13 cm) shape is a 2 in. (5 cm) shape.

10 From the base of the 5 in. (13 cm) shape hangs a 4 in. (10 cm) shape. Within this hangs a 2⅓ in. (6 cm) shape. Before attaching this to the top of the 4 in. (10 cm) shape, I added a short length of straw (½ in./12 mm) to allow it to hang lower.

11 From each corner of the 4 in. (10 cm) shape hangs a 1¾ in. (4.5 cm) shape. Again, I added a short length of straw before attaching.

12 Hanging from the base of the 4 in. (10 cm) shape, is a 2½ in. (6.5 cm) shape and, hanging from this, a 1¾ in. (4.5 cm) shape.

13 Attach a length of cotton to the top of the sculpture, for hanging.

10

11

construction diagram

GORGEOUS GEOMETRY

FOR SOME TIME NOW, THERE HAS BEEN A HUGE TREND IN GEOMETRICS IN THE DESIGN, INTERIORS, AND FASHION WORLD. IT IS EASY TO SEE WHY. THE CLEAN, GRAPHIC LINES OF GEOMETRIC SHAPES PROVIDE A COOL AND CONTEMPORARY LOOK THAT IS ADAPTABLE WITH ENDLESS COMBINATIONS. USE SOME COLORED PAPER AND WIRE TO CREATE THIS STYLISH MOBILE.

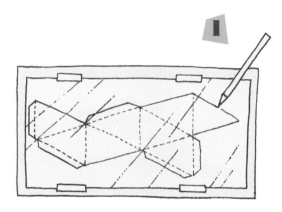

1 Trace out a shape from the templates. Lay the template on the back of a piece of colored paper or card stock (card) and secure with masking tape. Go over the lines using a sharp pencil, making sure to mark the folds with dotted lines, as shown on the template.

YOU WILL NEED

- *Tracing paper*
- *Pencil*
- *Templates, page 141*
- *Colored paper or thin card stock (card)*
- *Masking tape*
- *Scissors*
- *Ruler*
- *Knife or similar, for scoring*
- *Craft glue*
- *Needle*

- *Florist's wire cut into (7 in.) 18 cm lengths*
- *Small bullnose pliers*
- *Length of ¼ in. (6 mm) doweling measuring 12 in. (30 cm)*
- *String or thread, for hanging*

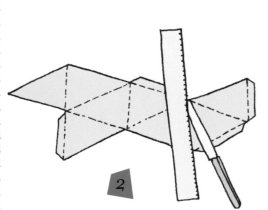

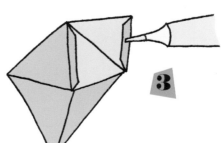

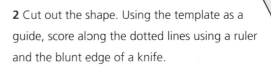

2 Cut out the shape. Using the template as a guide, score along the dotted lines using a ruler and the blunt edge of a knife.

3 Fold all the lines and glue flaps and you will be able to see the shape coming together. Place some glue along the outside edge of the glue flaps and stick them down to the inside of each corresponding edge to form the shape. Repeat this with the other template and make up several shapes in different colors.

4 Use a needle to pierce holes at the top and bottom of one of the shapes. Thread one end of a length of wire though the two holes. Use pliers to bend and twist the wire to secure.

5 Make similar holes in the next shape and thread with the opposite end of the wire used in Step 4. Secure in the same way. You want to leave about 1¼ in. (3 cm) between each shape. Trim off any spare bits of wire.

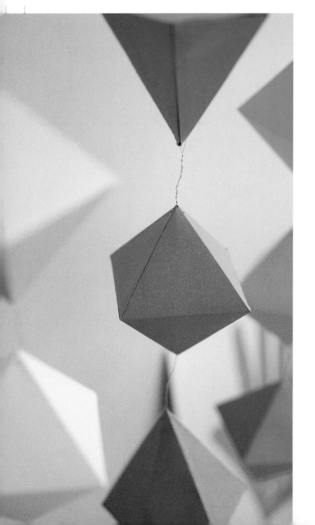

6 To secure a length of wire to a shape with a flat base, fold one end of the wire a couple times to make a T-shape. Make a hole in the center of the flat base. It will need to be slightly bigger than the ones you made in Step 4. Gently push the T-shape into the hole—you will need to bend it in line with the wire you are pushing in. Once in, gently jiggle the wire about a bit. It shouldn't come back through the hole.

7 Follow Steps 4 to 6 to make three strands of different shapes. When you come to the last shape on each strand, leave the final length of wire long.

8 Wind the top wire of each strand around the piece of doweling, placing one strand at the center and one at each end.

9 Tie a length of thread or string to either end of the doweling, for hanging.

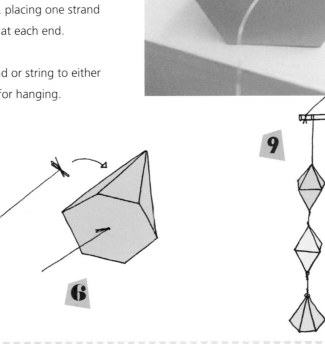

Abstract Copper and Wood

This stylishly simple mobile is made from copper foil and wood veneer. Copper foil is easy to work with—it is soft enough to cut with scissors and the surface is easily embossed. The cut edges are sharp, however, so take care. This mobile offers the perfect opportunity to experiment with different shapes and balance. I have used a thin slat of wood for hanging, having drilled holes for tying on the strands of shapes. If you prefer not to use a drill, tie the thread around a length of doweling or a twig, instead.

1 Trace out the shapes for the copper pieces. Lay the trace down on the copper foil and secure with masking tape. Go over the lines using an old ballpoint pen. Cut out the shapes using scissors and use a craft knife to cut any internal shapes. Be sure to protect your work surface with a cutting mat.

YOU WILL NEED

- *Templates, page 139*
- *Tracing paper*
- *Pencil*
- *1-mm thick copper foil*
- *Masking tape*
- *Old ballpoint pen (one with no ink)*
- *Scissors*
- *Craft knife*
- *Cutting mat*
- *Embossing tools*
- *Metal ruler*
- *Wood veneer*

- *Awl (bradawl) or similar, for piercing holes*
- *Nylon thread*
- *Wire cutters*
- *Copper florist's wire*
- *Jewelry pliers*
- *Drill (optional)*
- *Wooden baton measuring approximately 12 x ¾ x ¼ in. (30 x 2 x 0.5 cm)*
- *Matchsticks*
- *Waxed cotton*

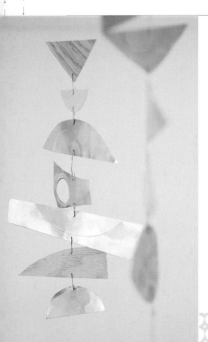

2 Emboss the surface of some of the shapes. Using the old ballpoint pen, draw around something circular—such as a cotton spool for the small circles and a glass for larger semicircles. Experiment on some spare bits of foil first. Simple lines drawn across a shape using a ruler work well, too.

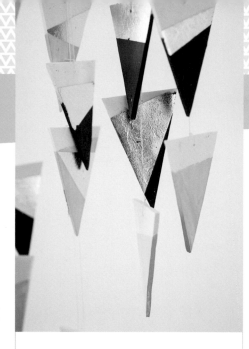

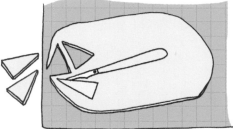

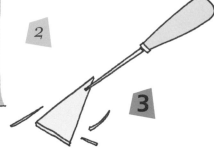

SHIMMER ARROWHEADS

I have chosen one of my favorite color combinations for this arrowhead mobile, but you can make it using any colors you like. The addition of silver leaf adds an eye-catching shimmer to this pretty and delicate design.

YOU WILL NEED

- *Template, page 139*
- *Tracing paper*
- *Pencil*
- *Small scrap of thin card stock (card)*
- *Scissors*
- *Cutting mat*
- *White, lightweight polymer clay*
- *Rolling pin*
- *Craft knife*
- *Ruler*
- *Awl (bradawl) or similar, for making holes*
- *Masking tape*
- *Acrylic paint*
- *Paintbrush*
- *Silver leaf*
- *Spray adhesive*
- *Twig*
- *Thread*

1 Trace out the template and transfer it to a piece of thin card stock (card) (see page 137). Cut this out.

2 Place the clay on to a cutting mat and roll out to a thickness of approximately ⅛ in. (3 mm). Use the template and craft knife to cut out lots of triangles. Leave these to dry or, if your clay is the type that needs to bake in the oven, follow the manufacturer's instructions for use.

3 Once the clay is hard or baked and cooled, use a ruler and craft knife to trim the triangles and sharpen up the edges. Use the awl (bradawl) to make a hole in the center of each triangle, approximately ½ in. (6 mm) from the top point.

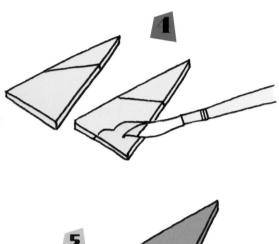

4 Cut strips of masking tape to tape across the top section of each triangle. Do this at different angles to vary the geometric shapes. Extend the tape around the edges and on to the back of the shape. Paint the unmasked sections in whatever colors you like. Paint the front and the sides of each shape first and wait for these to dry before turning over to paint the back.

5 Cut out triangles of silver leaf. Give the silver leaf side a thin coat of spray adhesive. Always follow the manufacturer's instructions when using spray adhesive. Lay the silver leaf in position on the shape and rub down before removing the backing paper. Trim off any bits of spare silver leaf.

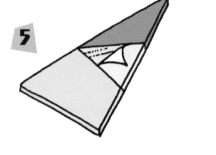

6 Paint the twig white. Attach a different length of thread to each triangle, using double lengths of thread for extra strength. Tie each length to the twig, starting at the center with the longest thread (mine measured approximately 25½ in. (65 cm). Gradually make the lengths of thread shorter as you move along the twig in each direction. This makes a nice arrow-shaped mobile.

7 Tie a length of string to each end of the twig, for hanging.

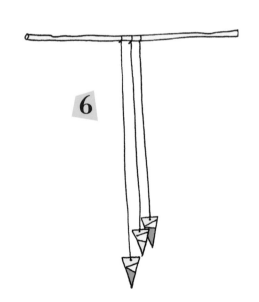

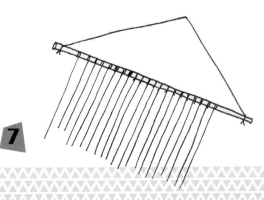

Geometric Stars

At the center of each beautiful star in this mobile is an icosahedron—a geometric shape with 20 triangular faces—and I have attached a point to each face. They make stunning geometric decorations for hanging. Each takes a bit of time to cut, fold, and stick, but the result is worth it.

YOU WILL NEED

- Templates, page 141
- Tracing paper
- Pencil
- Thin card stock (card)
- Masking tape
- Pin
- Ruler
- Craft knife
- Cutting mat
- Knife, or similar, for scoring
- Strong, quick-drying glue
- Embroidery floss (thread)
- Florist's wire
- Wire cutters

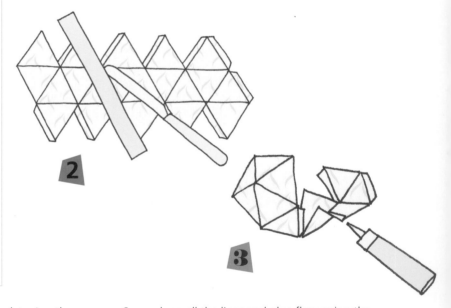

1 Trace out the icosahedron template. Lay the tracing paper over the reverse side of your card stock (card) and secure with masking tape. Use a pin to prick through each of the corner points. Follow the template to join up the points using a ruler and a pencil.

2 Using a craft knife, and protecting your work surface with a cutting mat, cut out the shape. Score along all the lines and glue flaps using the blunt edge of a knife.

3 Fold the scored lines, one by one, to form the 3-D shape. Apply glue to each flap—one at a time—and secure in position. This makes the icosahedron shape that forms the center of the star.

4 Trace out the shape for the point and transfer it on to card stock (card) using the pin method described in Step 1. Cut this out. You will need 20 of these.

5 Score along all the lines and fold each piece into a pyramid shape, securing the side flap with glue.

6 Fold in the flaps at the base and glue the point to one triangular face of the icosahedron.

7 Repeat with the remaining 19 pieces, building up one point at a time, until the star is complete.

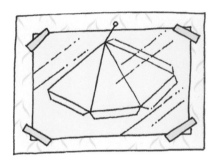

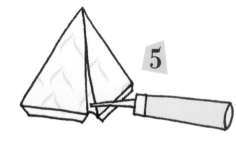

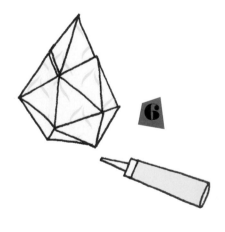

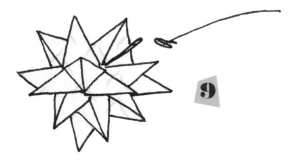

8 Follow Steps 1 to 7 to make a second star. Enlarge the template by 20 or 30 percent to make it a different size.

9 To assemble the mobile, cut a length of embroidery floss (thread) measuring 4¾ in. (12 cm). Cut two ¾ in. (2-cm) lengths of florist's wire and attach one to each end of floss (thread). Use a pin to make a hole between two points in the larger star. Fold one of the wires in half and push it through the hole. Repeat with the smaller star and thread in the same way, using the wire at the opposite end of the floss (thread).

10 To hang, make a hole at the top of the large star—exactly opposite the hole at the bottom. Attach a small length of wire to a length of floss (thread), as in Step 9. Fold the wire in half and push it through the hole. Use the floss (thread) to hang the mobile, making a loop at the top so that you can hang it from a hook.

Party-time Sparkle

Celebrate in style with this simple, yet stunning mobile. Made from strips of paper that alternate sparkling silver with warm pastels, this is a decoration that screams, "let's party!" The method is so speedy that you could make some really long lengths to hang in a row for a dazzling wedding-photo wall.

YOU WILL NEED

- *Thin card stock (card) in mirror silver, white, and pastel colors*
- *Ruler*
- *Pencil*
- *Craft knife*
- *Cutting mat*
- *Sewing machine*

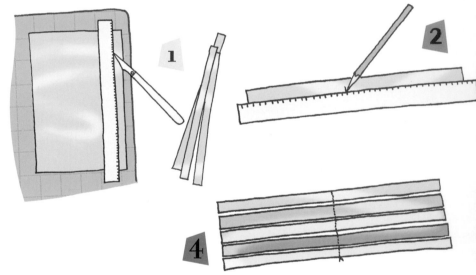

1 Cut strips of card stock (card) measuring 8¼ x ¾ in. (21 x 2 cm). Use a craft knife and protect your work surface with a cutting mat.

2 Mark the center point of each strip with a pencil.

3 Use a sewing machine to stitch down the central line of the first strip. Place the second strip alongside the first, aligning the side edges, and stitch along the central line to join the two strips together.

4 Keep adding strips in the same way, alternating the colors as you go.

5 Once you have achieved the desired length, simply leave enough thread at the top for hanging. Make a number of lengths in the same way, varying the width of the strips if you like.

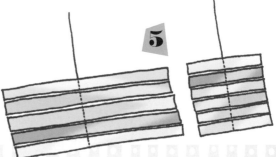

TWIST-AND-TURN DISKS

ACETATE IS A MAGICAL MATERIAL WHEN USED FOR MOBILES. IN THIS PROJECT, THE colors CONSTANTLY CHANGE AS THE DISKS TWIST AND TURN IN THE AIR. THEY OVERLAP EACH OTHER AND THE LIGHT THAT SHINES THROUGH THE PLASTIC CASTS brightly COLORED SHADOWS ON THE WALL.

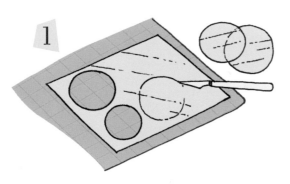

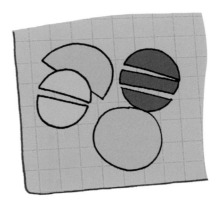

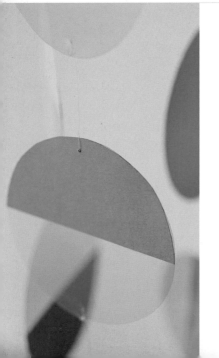

YOU WILL NEED

- *Letter-size (A4) sheets of acetate*
- *Craft knife*
- *Circle templates in different sizes*
- *Pencil*
- *Cutting mat*
- *Colored card stock (card)*
- *Ruler*
- *Craft glue*
- *Needle and nylon thread*
- *Scissors*
- *Metal ring*

1 Cut a number of acetate circles in different sizes. Use templates to do this, or simply draw around some circular objects. Use a craft knife for the cutting and protect your work surface with a cutting mat.

2 Cut a number of colored card stock (card) circles in different sizes. Snip some of these in half and cut others into strips of different widths.

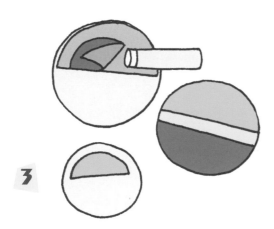

3

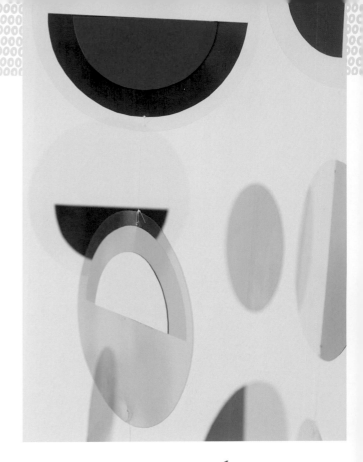

3 Use craft glue to stick the card stock (card) pieces on to the acetate disks. Be sure to vary the designs you make.

4 Arrange the acetate disks on a flat surface to make four columns in total. Mix up the sizes and move them around until you are happy with the combinations.

5 Thread a needle with nylon thread. Use the needle to pierce a hole through the bottom of the first disk in a column and then through the top of the second disk. Cut the thread and tie a knot to secure the two disks together. Make sure you have a ½-in. (1-cm) gap between the two disks.

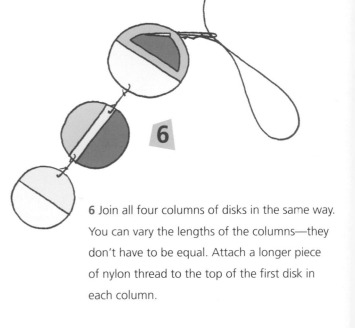

6

6 Join all four columns of disks in the same way. You can vary the lengths of the columns—they don't have to be equal. Attach a longer piece of nylon thread to the top of the first disk in each column.

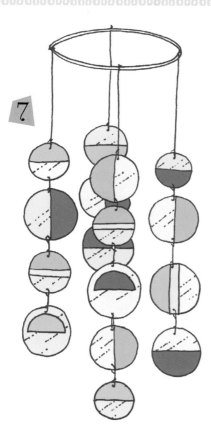

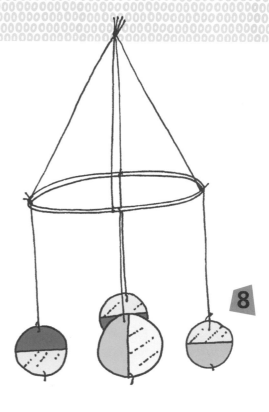

7 Tie each of the four columns of disks to the metal ring. Position them at quarter points on the ring, as shown. My columns hang 4¾ in. (12 cm) below the ring.

8 Cut four more lengths of nylon thread, each measuring 12 in. (30 cm). Attach these at the quarter points on the metal ring. Gather them together at the center—making sure that the mobile hangs straight—and tie a knot to join the four strands together. Trim off any uneven thread before hanging.

Festive Walnuts

When the nights start drawing in and Christmas produce begins to appear in the shops, grab a few walnuts to make this charming and festive hanging decoration. You could also use ivy or plain twigs, painted white, to hang the nuts.

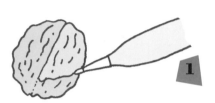

1 Use the silver felt-tip pen to paint one half of each walnut.

2 Tie a scrap of ribbon around each walnut, as shown, securing with a double knot. Trim the ends of each ribbon to ¾–1 in. (2–3 cm).

3 Take a twig measuring 16 in. (40 cm) long and bend it round into

a ring. Overlap the ends and use cotton thread to secure them.

4 Tie a length of colored thread to the knot of ribbon at the top of each walnut and attach the opposite end of the thread to the twig ring. Space the walnuts evenly around the ring and vary the lengths of colored thread.

YOU WILL NEED

- Silver felt-tip pen
- Walnuts
- Scraps of thin ribbon
- Scissors
- Twig, preferably with leaves
- Cotton thread
- Lengths of baker's twine or silver and gold thread

5 Cut two lengths of baker's twine or gold/silver thread, each measuring 16 in. (40 cm). Tie the ends of the first length of thread to opposite sides of the twig ring.

6 Rotate the twig ring by 90 degrees and repeat Step 5 with the second length of twine or thread, so that the two threads cross at the center.

7 Gather the two lengths of twine or thread at the center and tie together to make a loop for hanging.

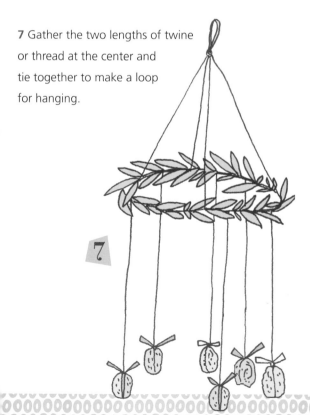

Fresh Flower Chandelier

YOU WILL NEED

- *Thick wire*
- *Tape measure*
- *Wire cutters*
- *Bullnose pliers*
- *Thin wire*
- *5 small glass bottles*
- *Fresh flowers*

The little bottles that feature in this project are easy to find if you look at online stores for flower arranging and wedding favors. Hung from a wire base and filled with a pretty mix of fresh flowers, they make a truly stunning decoration. Be sure to use thick wire—the bottles have water and can get heavy.

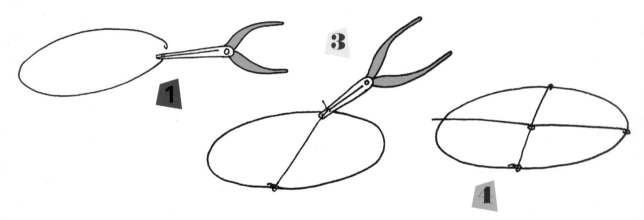

1 Cut a length of thick wire measuring 33 in. (84 cm). Bend the wire to form a ring and use pliers to bend a small loop at one end and a small hook at the other end. Place the hook into the loop, and squeeze together to secure.

2 Cut two lengths of thick wire measuring 1¼ in. (3 cm) more than the diameter of the ring you made in Step 1. Use pliers to wrap one end of the first wire around the wire ring—I started at the join.

3 Stretch the wire across the ring and wrap the opposite end around the ring. Trim off any extra wire.

4 Rotate the wire ring by 90 degrees and attach the second length of wire in the same way, so that the two wires cross at the center. Where the wires cross at the center, loop the second wire, around the first, to secure.

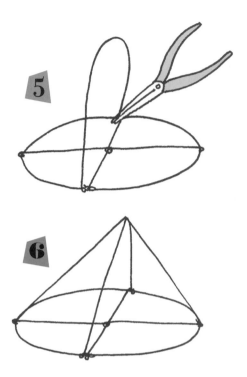

5 Now cut two lengths of thick wire measuring 20 in. (50 cm). Attach the ends to the same points on the wire ring that you attached the wires in Steps 2, 3, and 4.

6 Squeeze each wire at the center into a triangle shape.

7 Cut five varying lengths of thin wire that measure between 11 and 13½ in. (28 and 34 cm). Take one length of wire and use pliers to make a small loop at one end. Wrap the looped end of the wire around the top of a bottle, thread the opposite end of the wire through the loop, and pull tight.

8 Make a small loop at the opposite end of the wire, to hook over the wire ring. Repeat Steps 7 and 8 with all the other bottles.

9 Hook four of the bottles over the edge of the wire ring, placing them at those points where the hanging wires have been attached. Place the fifth bottle where the wires cross at the center of the ring.

10 Now for the fun! Pour a small amount of water into each bottle and arrange a pretty mini-bouquet of flowers in each one.

11 You can hang the mobile from a hook screwed into the ceiling.

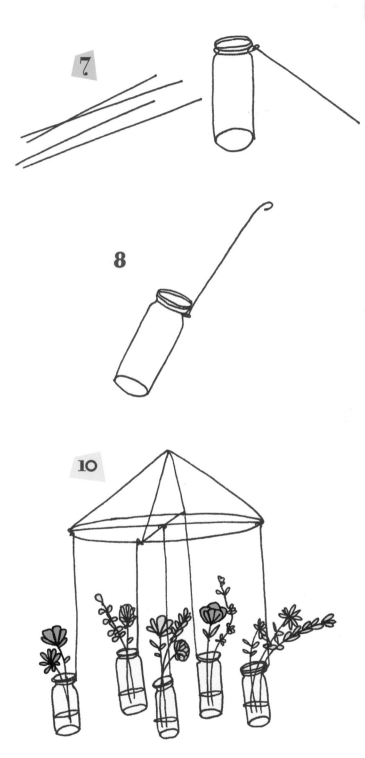

A Walk in the Woods

Turn a walk in the woods into a foraging expedition to provide materials for this nature-inspired mobile. It's a great project to get the kids involved in—they will love making found treasures into something special. Feathers, small pebbles, and seashells would work well, too.

YOU WILL NEED

- Selections of dried seedpods and leaves
- One twig
- Cotton thread or twine
- Florist's wire
- Wire cutters

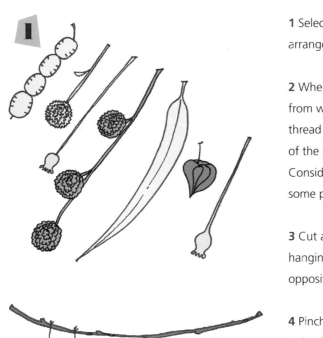

1 Select the seedpods and leaves you intend to use and arrange them in a row, considering their sizes and shapes.

2 When happy with the arrangement, select a long twig from which to hang the pieces. Cut a length of cotton thread or twine for each piece. Tie one end around the stem of the piece and the opposite end around the hanging twig. Consider the lengths of twine carefully—you may want some pieces balanced lower than others.

3 Cut a length of florist's wire that is twice the length of the hanging twig. Wind each end of the wire around an opposite end of the twig.

4 Pinch the wire at the center to form a triangle shape, and twist the point of the triangle into a loop for hanging.

CHERRY BLOSSOM CHEER

YOU WILL NEED

- *Pink and pale green tissue paper*
- *Ruler*
- *Pencil*
- *Scissors*
- *Craft glue*
- *Twigs*
- *Cotton thread*
- *Florist's wire*
- *Wire cutters*

Mobiles do not have to be complicated. Sometimes, even the simplest decoration can make a stunning focal point in a room. This stylish and pretty mobile has a Japanese look to it. It is very easy to make and will bring a little spring cheer to the gloomiest of winter days.

1 Cut a strip of pink tissue paper that measures 4¾ in. (12 cm) long by ⅔ in. (1.5 cm) wide. Cut a fringe all the way along the length of the strip, making the snips about 1⁄16 in. (2 mm) apart. Stop ¼ in. (5 mm) short of the top edge.

2 Run some glue along the uncut edge and roll the strip up. Pinch the glued section together and ruffle the fringed section, to make more of a flower shape.

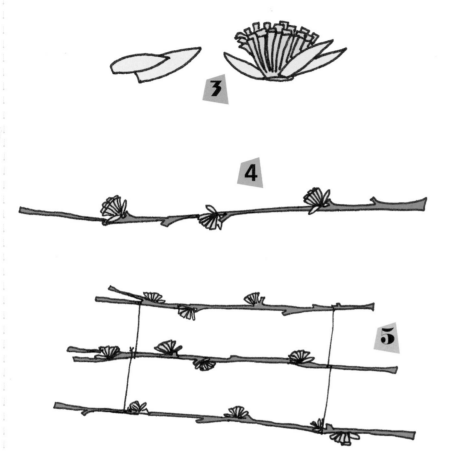

3 Cut some small leaf shapes from the pale green tissue. Dab glue at the end of a leaf shape and stick it to the bottom of the flower. You can add more leaves if you like. Make up several flowers in this way.

4 Cut three varying lengths of twig—it works well to have a longer length at the bottom. Glue tissue paper flowers along the lengths, at intervals.

5 Arrange the twigs one above the next and use cotton thread to tie them together, as shown. Make sure that the lengths of thread at each end of a twig are more or less the same.

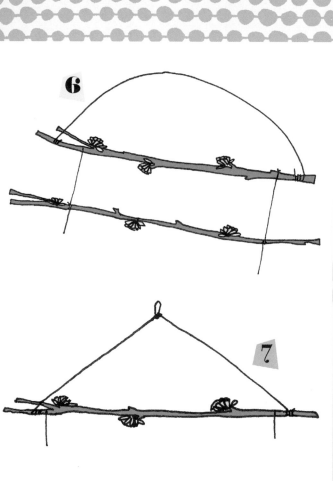

6 Now cut a length of florist's wire that measures twice the length of the top twig. Wind the ends of the wire around opposite ends of the twig.

7 Pinch the wire at the center to form a triangle shape, and twist the point of the triangle into a loop for hanging.

Little Hanging Pots

Macramé is back! I am a great collector of vintage craft books and many of those published during the 1970s have sections showing the wonders that can be created from a length of string and a few knots! Look out for suitable pots in thrift stores or at yard sales. This set has a lovely Japanese look to it. If your pots are different sizes, simply adjust the positions of the knots to fit.

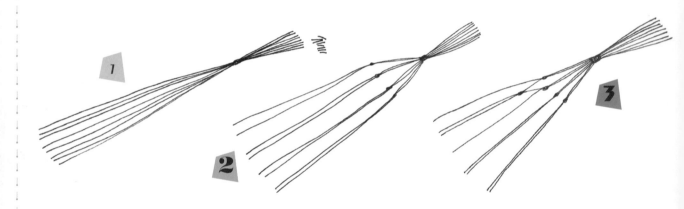

YOU WILL NEED

- *String*
- *Tape measure*
- *Scissors*
- *Small plant pots—mine measure 2⅓ x 2⅓ in. (6 x 6 cm)*
- *Small plants*

1 Cut eight lengths of string measuring 30 in. (75 cm). Gather the lengths together and tie a knot 6 in. (14 cm) in from one end. Trim off any uneven ends to make a neat tassel.

2 Divide the eight strands into four groups of two. Tie a knot in each pair of strands, 1¼ in. (3 cm) along from the top knot.

3 Now take one strand from each of two adjacent pairs and tie a knot 1½ in. (4 cm) along from the knot made in Step 2.

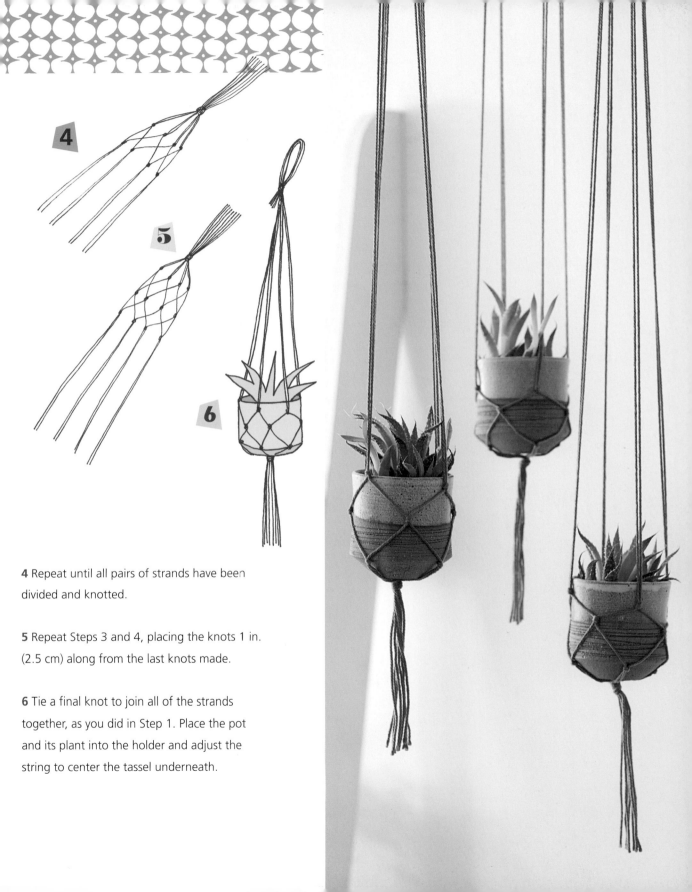

4 Repeat until all pairs of strands have been divided and knotted.

5 Repeat Steps 3 and 4, placing the knots 1 in. (2.5 cm) along from the last knots made.

6 Tie a final knot to join all of the strands together, as you did in Step 1. Place the pot and its plant into the holder and adjust the string to center the tassel underneath.

CHILDREN'S DELIGHTS

SAil AwAy

This combination of pale wooden boats and pretty paper sails makes a charming mobile for a child's bedroom. Wood veneer is readily available from craft suppliers. You have to be careful cutting it, to prevent it splitting, but it is worth the effort. It gives these little boats an authentic feel. I have made my hoop from plywood but you could use a ready-made one if you like.

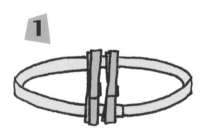

1 To make the hoop, soak the strip of plywood in some water for approximately half an hour. Bend it to form a circle, overlapping the ends, and use some clothespins (clothes pegs) to clamp it in this position. When it has dried, apply some wood glue to the overlapping ends and pin again while the glue dries.

YOU WILL NEED

- 1/16-in. (1-mm) thick strip of plywood measuring 23½ x ½ in. (60 x 1.3 cm)
- 2 clothespins (clothes pegs)
- Wood glue
- Template, page 139
- Tracing paper
- Pencil
- Wood veneer (thin enough to cut with a craft knife)

- Craft knife
- Cutting mat
- Patterned paper
- Ruler
- Nylon or cotton thread
- Scissors
- Masking tape
- Craft glue

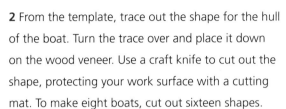

2 From the template, trace out the shape for the hull of the boat. Turn the trace over and place it down on the wood veneer. Use a craft knife to cut out the shape, protecting your work surface with a cutting mat. To make eight boats, cut out sixteen shapes.

3 Trace out the shape for the sail. Transfer it onto some patterned paper and cut it out using a craft knife. Use a ruler to keep your lines straight. Make eight sails in total.

4 Cut varying lengths of thread. I made my longest approximately 35½ in. (90 cm) and the shortest 15¾ in. (40 cm). Align a length of thread, vertically, in the center of one of the wooden hulls, as shown. Secure with a piece of masking tape and hold it up by the thread to check that the boat hangs straight. Adjust the position of the thread as necessary. Apply wood glue to the surface of one hull and stick a second hull over the first, aligning the edges and sandwiching the thread in between. Trim off any thread that may be poking out. Repeat to make the remaining hulls.

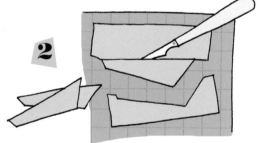

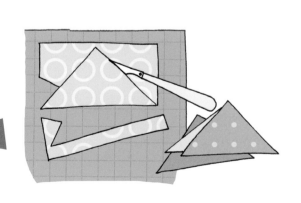

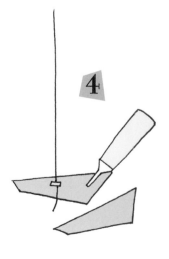

5 Fold the sail in half vertically, and spread craft glue over one half on the inside. Fold the sail around the thread making sure that the it runs along the fold and leaving a gap of approximately ⅓ in. (8 mm) between the hull and the bottom of the sail.

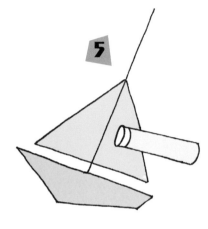

6 Tie the ends of the threads to the hoop you made in step 1, leaving 8 in. (20 cm) extra thread beyond the knot. Be sure to position the boats evenly around the circle and at different heights.

7 Choose four of the extra lengths of thread, spaced roughly at the quarterly points on the hoop. Gather them together and tie in a knot once you are satisfied that the mobile hangs straight. Trim off any lengths of thread that remain.

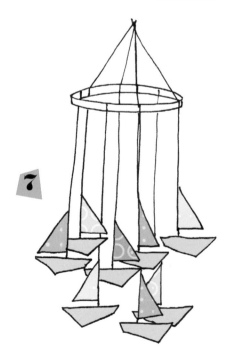

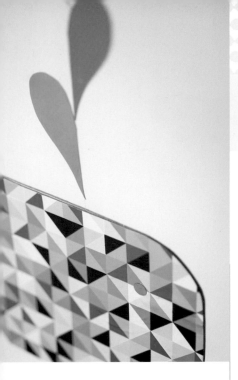

Spouting Whale

Watch this handsome beast swim above the bobbing waves as he spouts a fountain of colorful water droplets. I used a sheet of recycled giftwrap for the body of my whale. The color combinations seemed to fit perfectly. Whatever you choose—stripy, polka-dotted, or covered in flowers—you can guarantee this whale will be well loved!

YOU WILL NEED

- *Craft glue*
- *Gray board measuring 12½ x 13½ in. (32 x 34 cm)*
- *Patterned paper measuring 12½ x 13½ in. (32 x 34 cm)*
- *Templates, page 143*
- *Tracing paper*
- *Pencil*
- *Masking tape*
- *Craft knife*
- *Cutting mat*
- *Nylon or cotton thread*
- *Thin card stock (card) in a variety of colors*
- *Scissors*
- *Doweling measuring 4⅓ in. (11 cm)*

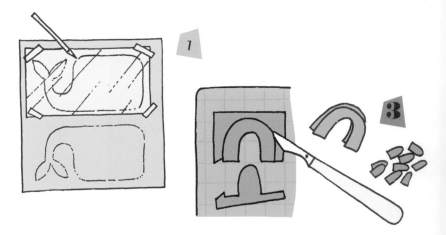

1 Spread craft glue over the piece of gray board and cover with patterned paper.

2 From the templates, trace out the shape of the whale, turn the trace over and position it on the non-patterned side of the card. Secure with masking tape and go over the lines with a sharp pencil. Turn the trace over and repeat to make a

second shape. Cut these out using a craft knife and protect your work surface with a cutting mat.

3 Trace out the templates for the waves and transfer to the colored card stock (card) (see page 137). Cut out ten shapes of each size, using different colored card stock (card) for the different sized pieces.

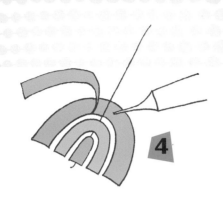

4 Assemble the wave sections. Place three waves—one of each size and one inside the other—with their flat edges at the bottom aligned. Cut a length of thread measuring 4¾ in. (12 cm). Dab glue over each wave and lay one end of the thread over the glue, running vertically through the center of the wave shape, as shown. Place a second set of waves over the first to secure. Repeat with the remaining sets of waves using another two threads measuring 4¾ in. (12 cm) and two measuring 7 in. (18 cm). Trim off any thread poking out at the bottom.

5 Trace out the templates for the water droplets and transfer to the colored card stock (card). Cut out five shapes. I made two in pink and three in orange.

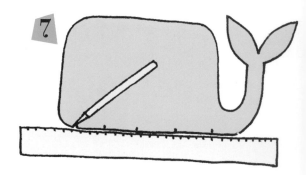

6 Fold the shapes in half vertically. Cut a piece of thread measuring 20½ in. (52 cm). Glue the inside of the droplet shape and fold the first one around the thread, leaving approximately 2 in. (5 cm) spare thread at the bottom. Make sure that the thread is running up the fold. Repeat with the next shape, sticking it above the first, but facing in the opposite direction. Continue with all the water droplets, alternating orientation as you go.

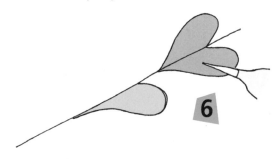

7 On the wrong side of one of the whale pieces, make a pencil mark at the center point along the bottom edge. Make two more marks ½ in. (1 cm) in from each side. Now mark the center points between the center and outer marks.

8 Use masking tape to stick the threads holding the waves to the inside of the whale. Use the shorter lengths at the first, middle and last pencil marks made in Step 7 and position them so that they measure 2¾ in. (7 cm) from the base of the whale to the bottom of the waves. On the remaining two pencil marks, the waves hang lower to 5½ in (14 cm).

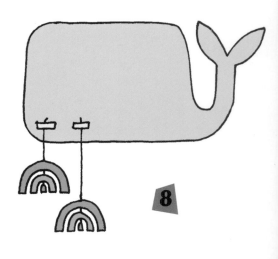

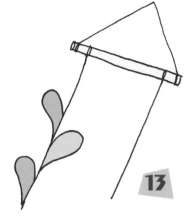

9 Along the top edge of the whale shape, position the thread with the water droplets 3 in. (8 cm) in from head end of the whale. Position a second length of thread—cut to the same length—2½ in. (6.5 cm) farther along from this. Secure both threads with masking tape.

10 Spread glue over the wrong side of one whale shape and position the second whale shape over the top, wrong sides facing and edges aligned. Place the whale under something heavy while the glue dries.

11 Cut out two small circles for the whale's eyes and glue one to each side of the head.

12 At the top of the whale shape, tie the two lengths of thread to the doweling, positioning the threads ½ in. (1 cm) in from each edge, making sure that the whale hangs straight before tightening the knots.

13 Cut a length of thread measuring approximately 12 in. (30 cm). Tie to each end of the doweling, for hanging.

Sleepy Elephants

These little sleepy elephants with their big flapping ears make a perfect mobile for the nursery. I chose a graphic gray fabric for the main body and a selection of brightly colored prints for the ears. You can match the fabrics to the color scheme of your room.

YOU WILL NEED

- Template, page 138
- Tracing paper
- Pencil
- Scissors
- Gray fabric for the main body: 24 x 20 in. (60 x 50 cm) is ample for eight elephants
- Pins
- Dressmaker's pencil or air-erasable pen
- Scraps of colored fabrics
- Iron
- Fiberfill (soft-toy stuffing)
- Needle and cotton thread
- Dressmaker's pencil or air-erasable pen
- Embroidery needle and floss (thread)
- Strip of 2-in. (5-cm) wide fabric to cover the hoop
- Wooden hoop (I used the inner part of a 7 in. (18 cm) embroidery hoop)
- Craft glue

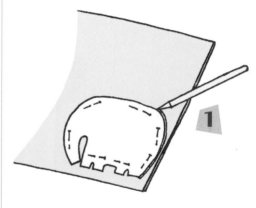

1 Trace the template of the elephant body and cut out. With right sides facing, fold the main body fabric in half. Pin the template to the folded fabric. Cut directly around the template or draw around it first using a dressmaker's pencil or air-erasable pen. Cut out pairs of elephants— I made seven in total.

2 Repeat Step 1 to cut ears from the colored fabric scraps. For seven elephants you need 14 pairs of ears.

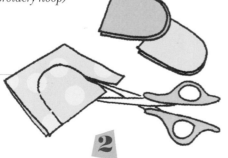

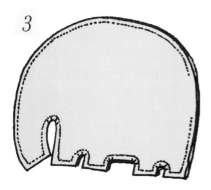

3 With right sides facing, pin the back and front of an elephant together. Sew around the edge with a small seam allowance and leaving a 1½ in. (4 cm) gap in the seam at the back of the elephant. Clip into the curves of the seam and turn the right way out. You may need to use a small paintbrush to push out the trunk and legs. Repeat to make all the elephants.

4 With right sides facing, pin a pair of ears together. Sew all around the curve of the ears leaving the straight edge open. Clip the curves, turn the right way out and press. Repeat to make all the ears.

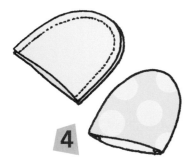

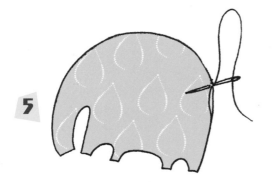

5 Lightly stuff the elephants with fiberfill (soft-toy stuffing) and sew up the gap in the seam using small stitches.

6 Fold in the raw edges on one of the ears and pin it in position on one side of an elephant. Use small stitches to attach it to the body. Turn the elephant over and sew on another ear in the same way. Repeat to sew on all the ears.

7 Use a dressmaker's pencil or an air-erasable pen to draw on the eyes. These are elongated semicircles. Use embroidery floss (thread) to sew the eyes using backstitch (see page 137).

8 To cover the hoop, cut a strip of 2-in. (5-cm) wide fabric that measures the diameter of the hoop with 1 in. (2 cm) extra. Glue the inside of the hoop. Fold over one long edge of the fabric strip and glue this to the inside of the hoop. When you get to the end fold under the raw edge by approximately ½ in. (1 cm) and stick down.

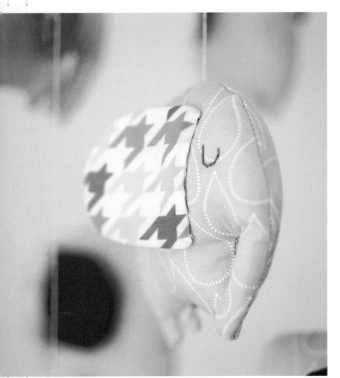

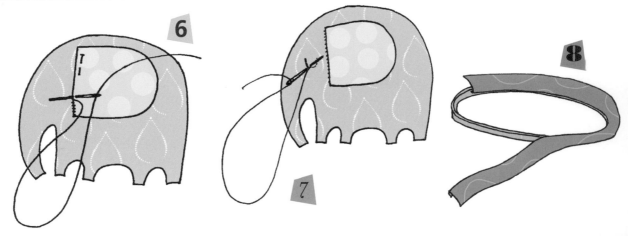

9 Fold over the other long edge of the strip. Glue the outside edge of the hoop and wrap the fabric over the top edge of the hoop. Glue over the fabric already stuck to the inside of the hoop and wrap the excess fabric over the bottom edge of the hoop to secure.

10 Sew a length of embroidery floss (thread) to the center of the elephant, along its back. If you do not want to see the knot, push the needle in ½ in. (1 cm) away from where you want the thread to be positioned, bring the needle out in the position, and pull the thread but not all the way through. Make a couple of small stitches at this point to secure.

11 Sew the opposite end of the floss (thread) on to the hoop. Repeat with all the elephants, positioning them evenly around the hoop and with different lengths of floss (thread).

12 Sew four lengths of embroidery floss (thread) to the top rim of the hoop, positioning each at a quarter point. Gather the four lengths of floss (thread) and tie a knot to join them together, making sure that the lengths are even and that the mobile hangs straight.

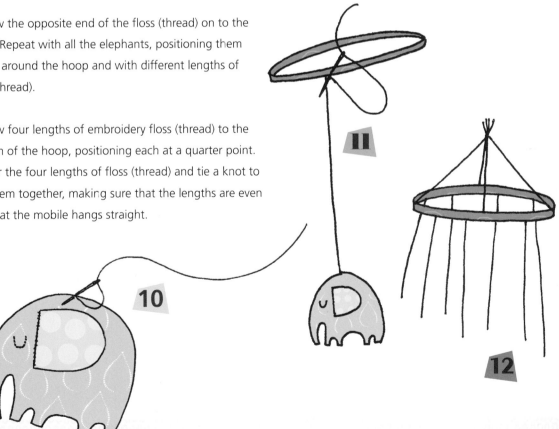

Folksy Felt Horses

I find inspiration for much of my work in folk art. These little felt horses were inspired by clay toys from the Russian village of Dymkovo, whose distinctive shapes are painted with bright-colored patterns. I have decorated mine with simple embroidery and have used tiny scraps of bright felt for the manes and tails. The pom-poms make a fitting finishing touch with an extra pop of color.

YOU WILL NEED

- Templates, page 138
- Tracing paper
- Masking tape
- Pencil
- Paper
- Scissors
- Pins
- Felt (main color plus scraps
- Air-erasable pen
- Embroidery needle and floss (thread) in different colors
- Card stock (card)
- Wool

1 Trace out the shapes for the horse's body, tail, ears, and mane and transfer to paper, securing with masking tape. Cut out the shapes to make templates.

2 Pin the horse template to the main color felt. Use an air-erasable pen to draw around the shape. Repeat to draw ten shapes in total and cut them out.

3 Use the templates to cut out five tails, ten ears and twenty mane sections.

Tip

If your felt has a right side and a wrong side (some wool felts do), be sure to draw five horse shapes facing one way and turn the template over to draw five facing the opposite way.

4 Take one horse body and, using the air-erasable pen, draw a series of joined-up loops across its width, as shown. Practice on paper first if you like, but don't worry if the loops are slightly different on each horse. This adds to their folksy charm!

5 Embroider the line of loops using a whipped backstitch, see page 137. If your hanging decoration is to be viewed from the front and back, embroider both sides of each horse in this way. If you only intend to embroider one side, decide which way you want the horses to face—I had mine facing opposite directions.

6 Use the air-erasable pen to draw on the eyes and embroider in the same way.

7 To make a pom-pom, cut a piece of card stock (card) measuring 1–1½ in. (3–4 cm) wide and wrap a length of wool around it 30 times. Slip the wool from the card. Tie one end of a longer length of wool around the middle of the wound wool and secure using a tight knot. Do not cut the length of wool. Snip the wool loops, as shown, and fluff up the fibers. Snip any loose ends to make a nice, neat ball. Make a number of pom-poms in this way—I made five.

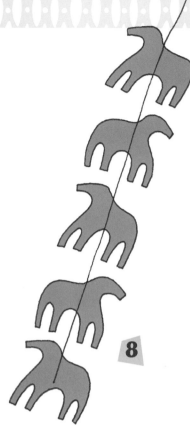

8

9 Position the tail, ears, and mane section on each horse, making sure they overlap the body of the horse by about ¼ in. (5 mm).

10 Place one remaining horse section over each of the first five and pin all around. When it comes to the bottom-most horse, gather the group of pom-poms together and place the ends of their wool ties so that they overlap the bottom edge of the horse before pinning.

8 To assemble the hanging, lay five horses on your work surface, wrong side up and one above the other. Cut a length of wool or embroidery floss (thread) and run it up the center of the horse shapes, from the bottom to the top, as shown. It should extend out above the top horse by 12 in. (30 cm). Use the illustration above as a guide for positioning the wool or floss (thread), to ensure that the horses hang straight.

11 When you have finished pinning, hold the decoration up by the string to see if the horses are straight. You may need to make a couple adjustments. Sew all around the edge of each horse, about ⅛ in. (3 mm) in from the edge. Tie a loop in the wool or floss (thread) at the top for hanging.

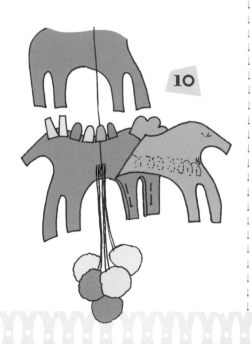

10

Sausage Dogs

I have a little dachshund called Otis. He is quite a character and I often use him as a model for a project. He has appeared on a cushion, as a softie, as a pull-along toy, and now in a mobile!

YOU WILL NEED

- Scissors
- Patterned paper
- Ruler
- White letter-size (A4) paper
- Pencil
- Tracing paper
- Templates, page 140
- Masking tape
- Craft knife
- Cutting mat
- Craft glue
- Black felt-tip pen
- Needle and embroidery floss (thread)
- Florist's wire
- Wire cutters
- Bullnose pliers

1 For each dog, cut a strip of patterned paper that measures the same as the short edge of a letter-size (A4) sheet of paper by 8⅔ in. (22 cm). Lay the patterned paper, right side up, on top of the white paper, aligning the short edges to one side. Photocopy the page so that you have a patterned sheet of paper with a white strip down one side. If you don't have access to a photocopier, stick patterned paper to the white paper using craft glue.

2 Trace out the shapes for the three different sausage dogs, their ears, and the bone.

3 Fold the photocopied sheet of paper in half. Place a template on the paper, aligning the straight edge with the fold, and making sure that the head is positioned in the white area. Secure with masking tape and transfer the shape on to the paper.

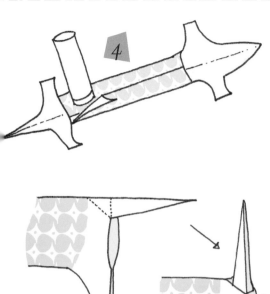

4 Using a craft knife, and protecting your work surface with a cutting mat, cut out the shape. Roll the shape into a tube, glue along one edge of the underbelly, and stick to the other side of the underbelly.

5 Make two creases at the base of the tail section, as shown. With finger and thumb, gently push the second crease so that it folds into, and under, the first crease. This will make the tail stick straight up in the air.

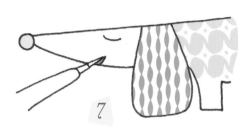

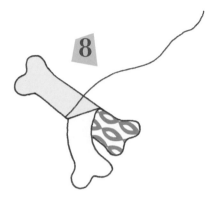

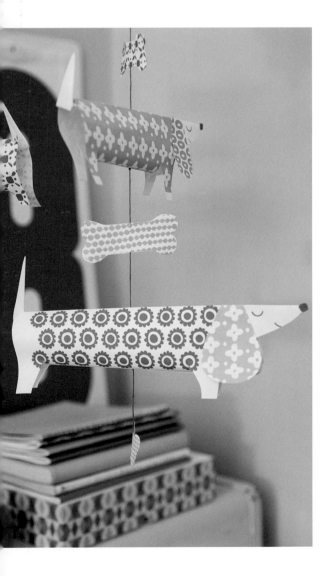

6 Repeat Steps 3, 4, and 5 to make several dogs. I made two big dogs, two medium-sized dogs, and one small dog. Also cut out five pairs of bones from different patterned paper, and five sets of ears.

7 For each dog, fold a set of ears in half and dab some glue in the fold. Position the ears on the dog's head. Stick a small circle of colored paper at the tip of each side of the head, to make a nose. Draw in the eyes and mouth with a black felt-tip pen.

8 Cut a length of embroidery floss (thread) measuring 21½ in. (55 cm) in length. Take a pair of bone shapes. Glue the wrong side of one shape and stick it to second shape, sandwiching the floss (thread) between them.

9 Tie a knot in the floss (thread), 2 in. (5 cm) from the bone. Thread the floss (thread) onto a needle and take the needle up through the inside of the dog, bringing the needle out at the fold directly above where you entered at the underbelly (see Tip).

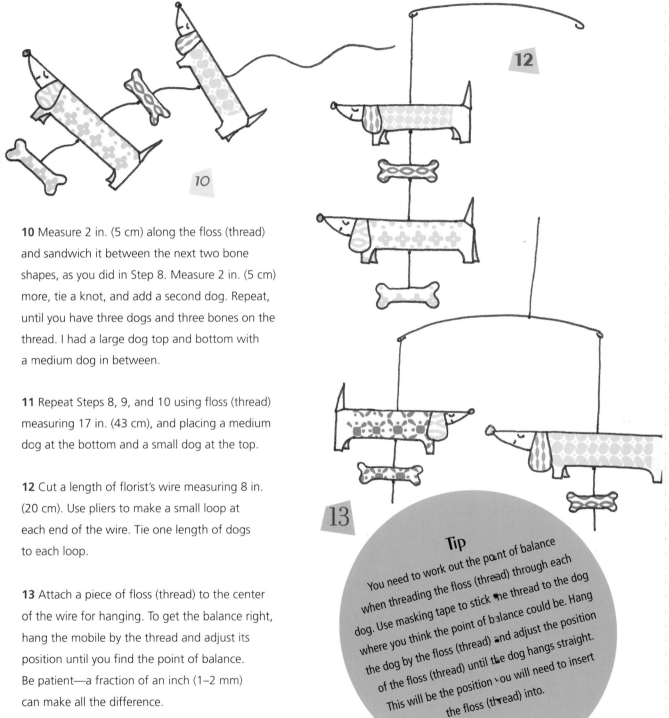

10 Measure 2 in. (5 cm) along the floss (thread) and sandwich it between the next two bone shapes, as you did in Step 8. Measure 2 in. (5 cm) more, tie a knot, and add a second dog. Repeat, until you have three dogs and three bones on the thread. I had a large dog top and bottom with a medium dog in between.

11 Repeat Steps 8, 9, and 10 using floss (thread) measuring 17 in. (43 cm), and placing a medium dog at the bottom and a small dog at the top.

12 Cut a length of florist's wire measuring 8 in. (20 cm). Use pliers to make a small loop at each end of the wire. Tie one length of dogs to each loop.

13 Attach a piece of floss (thread) to the center of the wire for hanging. To get the balance right, hang the mobile by the thread and adjust its position until you find the point of balance. Be patient—a fraction of an inch (1–2 mm) can make all the difference.

Tip
You need to work out the point of balance when threading the floss (thread) through each dog. Use masking tape to stick the thread to the dog where you think the point of balance could be. Hang the dog by the floss (thread) and adjust the position of the floss (thread) until the dog hangs straight. This will be the position you will need to insert the floss (thread) into.

Sky-bound Town

This mobile makes a lovely gift for a first birthday, its fluffy clouds, pretty houses, and little cars adding a charming decoration to any nursery. The small, colorful buttons used for making the wheels on the cars add a supersweet detail.

YOU WILL NEED

- *Tracing paper*
- *Pencil*
- *Templates, page 142*
- *Scissors*
- *Pins*
- *Fabric scraps*
- *Needle and cotton thread*
- *Fiberfill (soft toy stuffing)*
- *Iron*
- *Buttons*
- *2 lengths of balsa wood measuring ¼ x ¼ x 11 in. (0.5 x 0.5 x 28 cm)*
- *Wood glue*
- *½-in. (1-cm) eyehook*

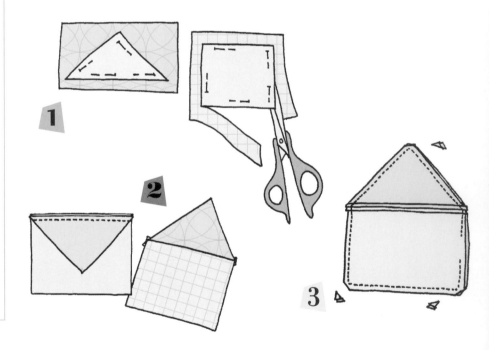

1 To make a little house, trace out a square and a triangle from the templates. Cut out the traces and pin to some fabric. Cut out two of each shape.

2 With right sides facing, align the base of a triangle with the top of a square. Sew a seam across and trim. Repeat with the two remaining shapes.

3 With right sides facing, place the back and the front of the house together. Pin and sew around the edge, leaving a 1½ in. (4 cm) gap in the seam. Trim the seam and cut across the corners, taking care to avoid any stitches.

4 Turn the house the right way out and press. Stuff loosely with fiberfill (soft toy stuffing).

5 Sew up the gap using small stitches. Repeat the steps to make three more houses. I made two thin-shaped houses and one each of the other sizes.

6 Trace the shape for the tree. Use this to cut back and front tree shapes and sew them together following Steps 3, 4, and 5.

7 Make two clouds in the same way.

8 Make three cars in the same way. Finish each one with two buttons on each side for the wheels.

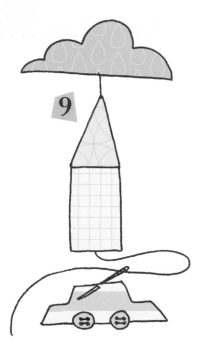

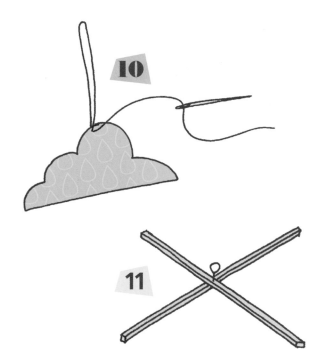

9 Use a needle and thread to sew a car to one of the houses leaving 2-in. (5-cm) gaps between the shapes. Make two like this. Make \up another column with a cloud, a house, and a car in the same way.

10 Stitch a loop of thread to the top of each column of shapes and the remaining cloud, house, and tree. Make the loops different lengths.

11 Take the two lengths of balsa wood and cross them at the center. Use wood glue to secure the wood where they overlap. Screw an eyehook into the upper strip of wood, at the center.

12 Slip the looped threads onto the balsa wood, spreading them out along the four spokes.

13 Tie a length of thread to the eyehook, for hanging. At this point you need to hold the mobile up by the hanging thread to check the balance. You will need to move the looped threads in different directions along the wooden spokes, until the balance is right.

BALANCING ACT

These jolly little acrobats hang from a trapeze and can be moved around to create endless combinations of circus high jinx. Hang them by their feet or by their hands, in groups, or all in a row. Although they feature in a chapter of mobiles for little ones, this is one of my personal favorites and is destined for a space above my desk!

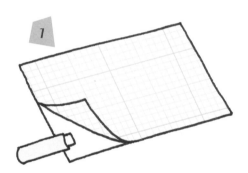

1 Use craft glue to stick a sheet of paper to each side of several sheets of thin card stock (card). I used lined and graph paper recycled from old schoolbooks. You need enough card stock (card) to make nine acrobats.

YOU WILL NEED

- Craft glue
- Letter-size (A4) lined and graph paper
- Letter-size (A4) thin card stock (card)
- Template, page 138
- Tracing paper
- Pencil
- Masking tape
- Craft knife
- Cutting mat
- Patterned paper
- Numbers (see method)
- Scissors
- Small hole punch
- Black felt-tip pen
- Colored string
- Length of 2-mm doweling measuring 12 in. (30 cm)

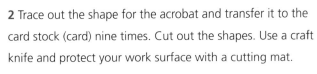

2 Trace out the shape for the acrobat and transfer it to the card stock (card) nine times. Cut out the shapes. Use a craft knife and protect your work surface with a cutting mat.

3 Trace out the shape for the hat and use this to cut 18 hat shapes from a mixture of patterned papers. Stick two hats on each acrobat—one at the front and one at the back.

4 You can print the acrobats' numbers from a computer or buy numbered stickers. I printed mine, making them ⅝ in. (16 mm) high on disks measuring 1 in. (25 mm) in diameter. Print out two of each number, cut them out using scissors, and glue to the front and back of the acrobats.

5 Use a small hole punch to make an eye for each acrobat and draw in a nice, curly moustache using a black felt-tip pen.

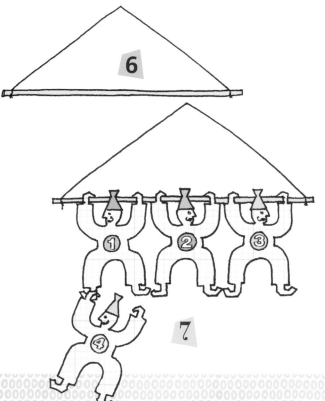

6 Cut a length of colored string measuring two and a half times the length of the doweling. Attach each end of the string to either end of the doweling, for hanging.

7 You can now hang a row of acrobats along the rod, hooking them on by their curved hands and feet. Add more of the little figures to complete the mobile, hooking their hands and feet together.

Wild West

If you are anything like me, you open presents very carefully in order to save the lovely wrapping paper. This funky, geometric wrap was in my paper stash and proved perfect for these little teepees. Bright-colored embroidery floss (thread) wrapped around the rustic-looking stick adds a textured detail to the theme.

YOU WILL NEED

- Craft glue
- Patterned paper
- Thin card stock (card) in different colors
- Templates, page 142
- Tracing paper
- Pencil
- Masking tape
- Scissors
- Cutting mat
- Craft knife
- Colored paper
- Embroidery floss (thread) in different colors
- Stick
- Needle and nylon thread

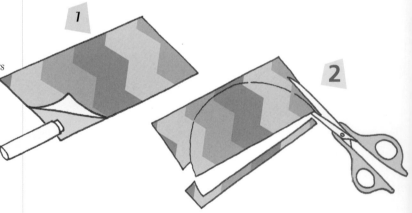

1 Glue a sheet of patterned paper to some colored card stock (card). You will need it to measure 8½ x 4 in. (21 x 10 cm).

2 Trace out the shape for the teepee and transfer onto the thin card stock (card). Cut out the shape using scissors.

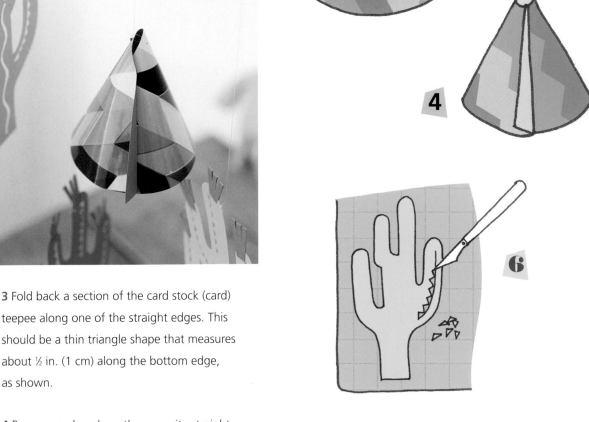

3 Fold back a section of the card stock (card) teepee along one of the straight edges. This should be a thin triangle shape that measures about ½ in. (1 cm) along the bottom edge, as shown.

4 Run some glue along the opposite straight edge, and bend the teepee into a cone shape. Overlap the folded-back edge with the glued edge, to secure.

5 Trace out the shapes for the cacti and transfer on to some green card stock (card)—I used three different shades of green. Cut out the shapes.

6 Protecting your work surface with a cutting mat, use a craft knife to cut shapes in the cacti. Follow the design on the templates for this, tracing them out if you like, although cutting freehand will add more variety, which looks good.

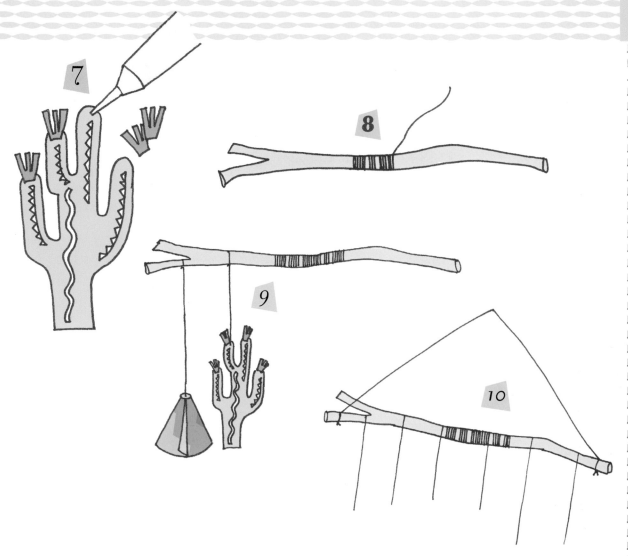

7 Trace out the shape for the cacti flowers and transfer onto colored paper. Here, again, you can cut these out freehand if you like. Stick them on to the tips of the cacti.

8 Wind some lengths of colored embroidery floss (thread) around the stick, securing the ends with a little glue. Vary the colors.

9 Use a needle to attach a length of nylon thread to each of the mobile shapes and tie them to the stick in a row. Space them out evenly and hang them at different heights.

10 Cut a length of embroidery floss (thread) that is two and a half times the length of the twig and tie to each end, for hanging.

NATURAL INSPIRATION

Birds of a Feather

The clean lines and subtle colors of this mobile give the piece a Scandinavian feel. A simple cutting and folding technique adds an interesting design element to the wings. Use paper that is white on one side and colored on the other, so that the 3-D effect really shows as the birds twist and turn in the air.

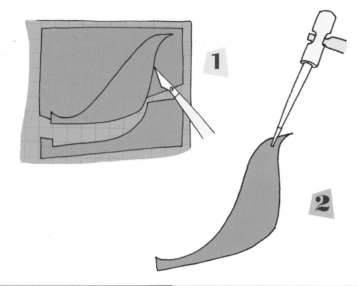

1 Trace out a bird shape from the template and transfer it to some card stock (card) (see page 137). Use a craft knife to cut out the shape, protecting your work surface with a cutting mat. Repeat to make a number of birds in the two different sizes. I made three the large ones and four small.

2 Use a hole punch to make the eyes. I used a smaller size punch for the smaller bird.

YOU WILL NEED

- *Template, page 139*
- *Tracing paper*
- *Pencil*
- *Masking tape*
- *Card stock (card) in different shades of gray*
- *Craft knife*
- *Cutting mat*
- *Small hole punch*
- *Colored paper that is white on the back*
- *Craft glue*
- *Two ⅕ in.² (5 mm²) balsa-wood batons measuring 11 in. (28 cm)*
- *Wood glue*
- *⅓-in. (10-mm) eyehook*
- *Scissors*
- *Nylon or cotton thread*

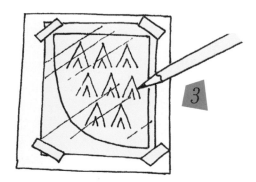

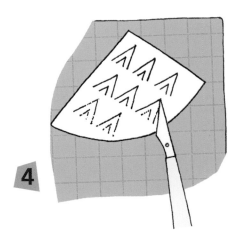

3 Trace out the shape for the wing. Turn the trace over and position it over the white side of the colored paper. Secure with masking tape and use a pencil to go over the lines on the trace. Turn the trace over and repeat to make a second wing. Make another six pairs of wings in all.

4 Use a craft knife to make cuts on the wings following the lines of the double triangles marked on the template. Push out and fold down each triangle.

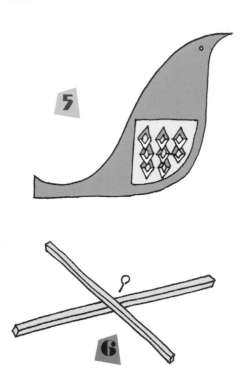

5 Apply craft glue to the white side of each wing and stick one on either side of the bird. Repeat this with all the other wings.

6 Take the two balsa-wood batons, place them across each other at the center, and glue together at this point, using wood glue. Screw an eyehook into the center as shown.

7 For each bird, make a small hole at the point marked on the template. Thread a length of nylon or cotton through the hole. Tie each to the strips of balsa, varying the lengths of thread.

8 Cut and tie a length of thread from the hook, for hanging. At this point you need to hold the mobile up by the hanging thread, to check for balance. Move the tied-on birds along the sticks in different directions until the balance is right.

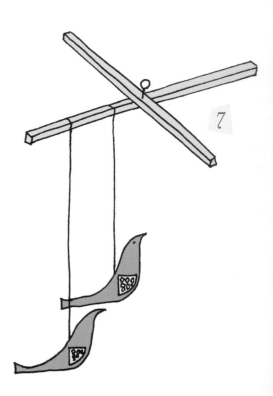

FESTIVE SNOWFLAKES

CHRISTMAS IS A GREAT TIME TO SHOW OFF YOUR CRAFTING SKILLS, WITH COUNTLESS OPPORTUNITIES FOR FILLING YOUR HOME WITH BEAUTIFUL HANDCRAFTED DECORATIONS. THIS GORGEOUS MOBILE IS MADE FROM DELICATE CURLS OF PAPER. PACK IT AWAY CAREFULLY EACH YEAR AND IT WILL BRING PLEASURE FOR MANY CHRISTMASES TO COME. ONCE YOU HAVE LEARNT HOW TO MAKE THE DIFFERENT SHAPES, YOU CAN MIX AND MATCH THEM ENDLESSLY. EACH SNOWFLAKE WILL BE UNIQUE!

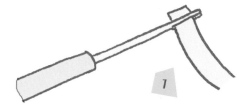

1 For shapes A, B, and C (see page 96), cut an 11-in. (28-cm) length of quilling paper. Place the end of the strip into the slot on the quilling tool.

2 Wind the paper tightly around the tool, until you reach the end of the strip.

YOU WILL NEED

- *White ¼-in. (6-mm) quilling paper*
- *Pencil*
- *Ruler*
- *Scissors*
- *Quilling tool*
- *Craft glue*
- *Nylon thread*
- *Colored string*

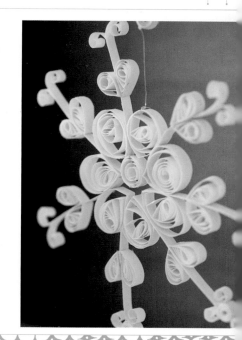

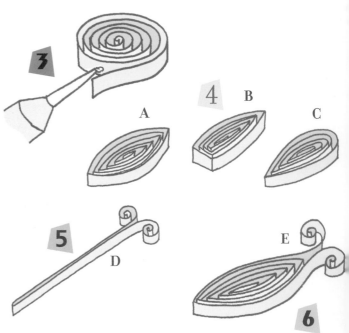

3 Release the end of the paper—letting it spring out—and ease it off the quilling tool. Dab a little craft glue at the end of the strip to secure the spiral shape you have made. When making a number of these spirals for a snowflake, try and get the circles all the same size.

4 To make shape A, pinch a spiral at the top and the bottom. Pinch the top and flatten the bottom for shape B. Pinch just the bottom for shape C. (To make shape C in the smaller size, cut the quilling paper to 7 in./18 cm).

5 To make shape D, cut the quilling paper to 7 in. (18 cm), and fold it in half. Place one of the ends in the quilling tool and twist it around a few times before releasing it. Repeat on the other side. Glue the folded strip together from the crease to the curls.

6 To make shape E, run glue along the folded strip on shape D and then wrap it around shape A, as shown.

7 To make shape F, cut the quilling paper to 7 in. (18 cm). Wind it tightly around the quilling tool. After releasing and easing from the quilling tool, rewind the strip tightly and glue the end to secure.

8 To make shape G, cut the quilling paper to 4¾ in. (12 cm). Fold it in half, run some glue around the edge of shape F, and center it within the glued strip. Wrap the strip tightly around shape F and glue the two sides together.

9 Follow the illustrations above to construct a number of snowflakes. It is best to arrange all the pieces first, and then to apply small amounts of glue where the shapes touch each other. On two of the designs, I have started with a spiral made following Steps 1 to 3.

10 Join the snowflakes together by tying some nylon thread from one flake to another. Loop a length of colored string through the top snowflake, for hanging.

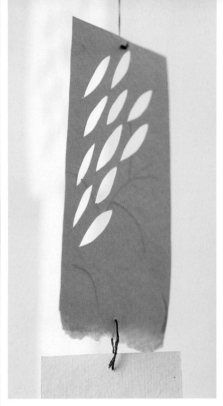

PRETTY PAPER

The success of this mobile lies in getting the balance exactly right. Once you have mastered this, you can make beautiful mobiles using a few basic materials and the minimum of effort. I have used Japanese handmade paper embedded with leaves and flowers to create a mobile that is charming in a simple and elegant way.

YOU WILL NEED

- Ruler
- Textured floral paper
- Craft knife
- Cutting mat
- Needle and embroidery floss (thread)
- Length of doweling measuring 21 in. (54 cm)

1 Measure several paper strips measuring approximately 2¼ in. (6 cm) in width—they can vary by ¾–1 in. (2–3 cm). Use a craft knife to cut them out, protecting your work surface with a cutting mat. Cut the strips into rectangles of varying length between 2¾ and 4½ in. (7 and 11 cm). You need about ten rectangles in total.

2 Use the craft knife to cut out a few shapes on some of the paper rectangles. These will add a pretty element when light shines through the mobile and casts shadows on the wall.

Tip

When cutting the paper rectangles, leave a few of the rough edges that you get with handmade paper, to add a little texture to the mobile.

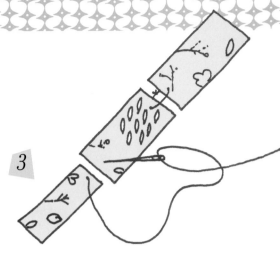

3

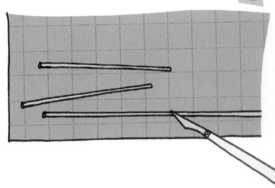

4

3 Arrange the paper rectangles into four columns. I placed two lots of three and two lots of two together. Thread a needle with some embroidery floss (thread)—I chose a dark pink color to complement the petals in the paper. Use the needle and floss (thread) to join the rectangles together, as shown, tying and cutting the floss (thread) to achieve a ½ in. (1 cm) gap between each pair of rectangles.

4 Cut three pieces of doweling, each measuring 7-in. (18-cm). You can use a craft knife for this.

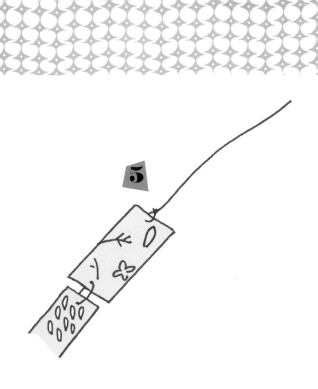

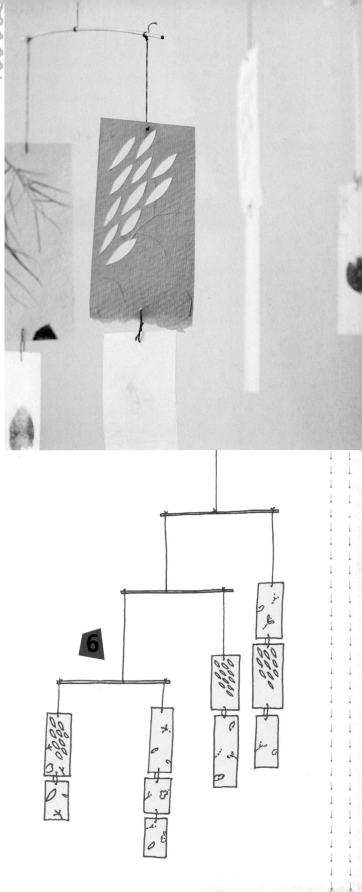

5 Use a needle and embroidery floss (thread) to attach a length of floss (thread) to the center top of each column of paper rectangles.

6 Follow the diagram to tie the columns to the doweling, starting with the lower section (note that the lengths of floss (thread) are shorter on this section than on the others). Tie a column of paper rectangles to each end of the doweling. Then tie a new length of floss (thread) around the center of the doweling and tie the opposite end of the floss (thread) to one end of the second section of doweling. Continue in this way to complete the arrangement. Finally tie a length of floss (thread) to the top section of doweling, for hanging. When you hold the mobile up by this last length of floss (thread) none of it will balance. You have to slide the floss (thread) along the sections of doweling until you achieve the balance.

Floral Filigree

This pretty and intricate mobile is easier to make than it looks. To show the delicate, sculptural design at its best, I have chosen to use paper that is white on one side and colored on the other. Once you know how to make the simple petals, there is no end to the different shapes and sizes that you can achieve. Mix and match them to create a hanging decoration that is truly unique.

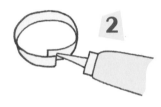

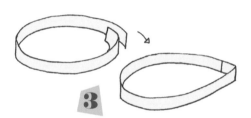

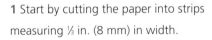

YOU WILL NEED

- Colored paper that is white on the back
- Pencil
- Ruler
- Scissors
- Craft glue
- Nylon thread

1 Start by cutting the paper into strips measuring ⅓ in. (8 mm) in width.

2 To make Flower A, cut a paper strip measuring 3½ in. (9 cm) in length. Curl it round to make a ring, overlap the two ends, and secure with craft glue.

3 Now cut seven more paper strips measuring 3½ in. (9 cm) in length. For each one, repeat Step 1 to make a paper ring, then pinch the top of each ring to make a petal shape.

4 Arrange the petals around the paper ring you made in Step 1. Secure the curved base of each petal to the ring using craft glue.

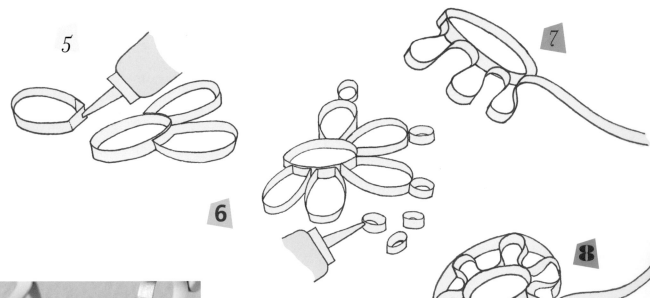

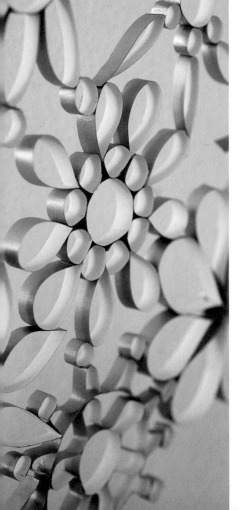

5 For Flower B, repeat Step 1 to make seven paper rings. Use six of the rings to make the petals. Do this by pinching the paper in two places per petal to make a flat base. Arrange the petals around the remaining paper ring, securing the flat bases to the ring using craft glue.

6 Now make six smaller paper rings from strips measuring 2 ⅓ in. (5.5 cm). Glue one to each of the six petals.

7 Repeat Step 1 to make a center ring for Flower C. Take a long strip of paper and glue one end to the center ring. Bend the paper strip to make a series of looped petals around the center ring, ½ in. (1 cm) apart, as shown, gluing each loop to the center ring to secure. Trim off any access paper. If you find that your strip of paper is not long enough, just add a second length to continue.

8 Run a strip of paper around the outside of the flower, to enclose the petal loops you made in Step 7. Use glue to secure the paper strip to each loop.

9 Repeat Step 7 to make another round of looped petals, this time making the loops slightly smaller.

10 To complete Flower C, repeat Step 6 to make a number of small paper rings and glue one to the top of each looped petal.

11 Use the above techniques to make any number of flowers, in any size, and with varying numbers of petals.

12 Lay the flowers on a flat surface and arrange them in a group so that each joins to another to make one big shape. Dab some glue where the petals of one flower meet the petals of another, to secure.

13 When the glue is dry, you should be able to lift the whole structure from one flower at the top of the piece. Attach a length of nylon thread to the top flower, for hanging.

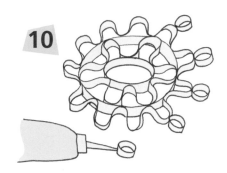

COPPER LEAVES

Celebrate the season changing from summer to fall with this delicate and pretty mobile. A long-time fan of silver leaf, I recently discovered a copper version, and I love it! Here, I have used pages from an old book as a backing—pale and faded paper makes a lovely contrast to shimmering copper. Hang this mobile in the corner of a room to bring the beautiful shades of fall into your home.

YOU WILL NEED

- *Templates, page 138*
- *Tracing paper*
- *Pencil*
- *Scissors*
- *Pages from an old book*
- *Spray adhesive*
- *Copper leaf*
- *Craft knife*
- *Cutting mat*
- *Needle and cotton thread*
- *Length of ¼-in. (6-mm) doweling measuring 10 in. (25 cm)*
- *Copper wire measuring 12 in. (30 cm)*

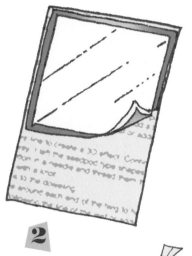

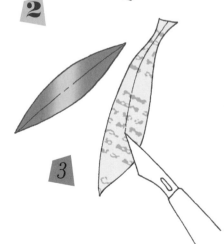

1 Trace the different leaf shapes and cut them out using scissors.

2 Lightly coat a book page with spray adhesive. Always follow the instructions when using spray adhesive. Lay the copper leaf over the top of the page, with the backing paper facing up. Rub down then remove the backing paper. Lay a piece of tracing paper over the page and rub down some more.

3 With the page side turned face up, use the templates you made in Step 1 to draw some leaf shapes. Cut these out. Using a craft knife, and protecting your work surface with a cutting mat, score each leaf from tip to tip. Don't cut all the way through, but use the very tip of the craft knife to break the surface of the paper. This may take some practice. On some leaves, give a slight curve to the score line.

4 Fold each leaf along the score line to create a 3-D effect. Leave the asymmetrical shapes flat.

5 Use a needle to thread a length of cotton through the top of each leaf and secure with a knot.

6 Tie the opposite end of each thread to the piece of doweling, hanging the leaves at different heights.

7 Attach a length of copper wire to the doweling, as shown, for hanging.

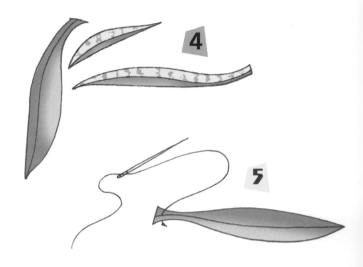

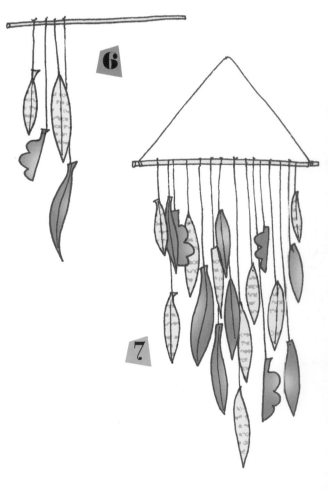

Birds in Flight

Sometimes you can really surprise yourself when working with paper. Simple shapes cut from a few scraps of white and colored paper can transform into gorgeous hanging decorations. These pretty swallows with cut-paper wings don't take long to make and will look charming wherever you choose to hang them.

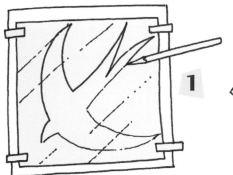

1 Make a trace from the template. Transfer the trace for the bird shape on to some thick white paper and cut it out.

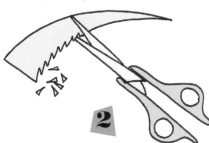

2 Transfer the traces for the two inner wing shapes onto thin colored paper and cut them out. Snip slanted triangle shapes all along the inner curved edge of each wing shape.

YOU WILL NEED

- *Template, page 139*
- *Tracing paper*
- *Masking tape*
- *Pencil*
- *Thick white paper*
- *Thin colored paper*
- *Small, sharp-pointed scissors*
- *Craft knife*
- *Cutting mat*
- *Craft glue*
- *Small hole punch*
- *Nylon thread*

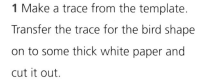

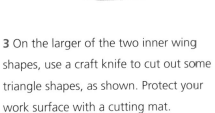

3 On the larger of the two inner wing shapes, use a craft knife to cut out some triangle shapes, as shown. Protect your work surface with a cutting mat.

4 On the smaller inner wing shape, run the blade of a craft knife along the length of the wing, ¼ in. (5 mm) in from the outer edge. Cut small triangles all along the slit, as shown.

5 Taking the craft knife, and following the guide on the template, score two lines that extend from the center of the bird down to the tips of the tail, as shown. Use the very tip of the blade to score the lines, making sure that the blade just breaks the surface of the paper.

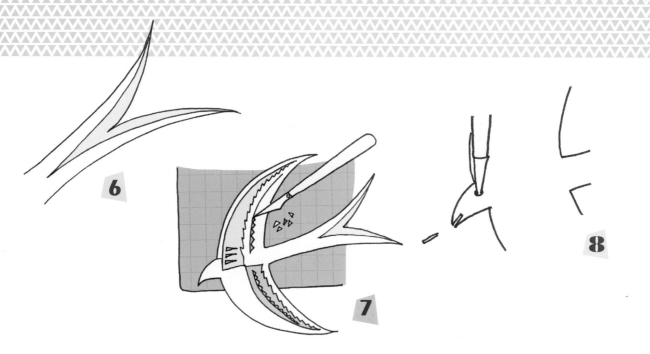

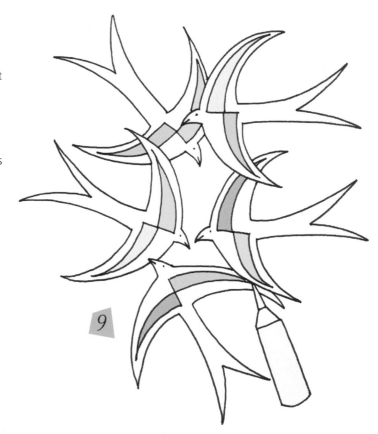

6 Crease along the score lines you made in Step 5 to give a 3-D effect to the bird's tail.

7 Use craft glue to stick the colored wing shapes to the main body of the bird. Repeat Step 4 to cut a row of triangles below the larger wing shape.

8 Use a small hole punch to pierce the bird's eye and cut a small slit for its beak.

9 Follow Steps 1 to 8 above to make a number of birds in the same way—I made five. Lay the birds on a flat surface and arrange them so that they overlap here and there. Glue them together at these points.

10 Loop a length of nylon thread through the cut-out section of the top bird, for hanging.

Tassels and Beads

Look out for strings of beads in thrift stores and at yard sales. They can cost next to nothing and, combined with some pretty paper tassels and mini fans, can make a pretty and original hanging decoration.

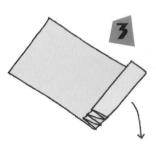

1 To make a paper tassel, cut a strip of paper measuring 7 ½ x 1 ¼ in. (19 x 3 cm). Cut snips into the long edge—all the way along and ⅛ in. (3 mm) apart. Stop ½ in. (1 cm) short of the top edge.

2 Run some glue along the uncut edge of the strip and roll the paper tightly. Make about 15 tassels this size and one tassel from a strip of paper measuring 7 ½ x 4 in. (19 x 10 cm).

3 To make a fan, cut a strip of paper measuring 51 x 1 ¼ in. (130 x 3 cm). Fold back and forth along the strip, making concertina folds approximately ¼ in. (5 mm) apart. Trim off any spare paper at the end. Open up the strip and run some glue along the top inside edge. Fold it up again and squeeze at the top to secure. Make about 15 fans in this way.

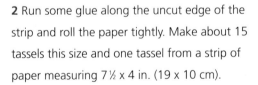

4 Use the awl (bradawl) to make a hole right through the top section of each fan and tassel, positioning it approximately ³⁄₁₆ in. (4mm) down from the top.

5 To make the larger of the two beaded hoops in this mobile, cut a length of wire measuring 14½ in. (37 cm) and use pliers to make a small loop at one end.

6 Thread a tassel onto the length of wire, pushing it down to the loop at the end. Now thread on some beads and a paper fan. Make sure that the patterned side of the fan faces outward. Continue threading beads, tassels, and fans on to the wire, with ¾ in. (2 cm) of beads between any two paper decorations.

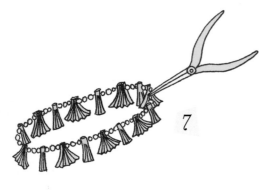

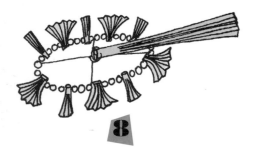

7 Finish off with beads and leave enough wire to make a small loop in the end. Bend the wire around to form a hoop and hook the two looped ends together. Squeeze the join using pliers, to secure.

8 Repeat Steps 5, 6, and 7 to make the smaller hoop using wire measuring 12 in. (30 cm). Tie a length of nylon thread across the diameter of the hoop and secure with a knot at each end. Tie a second length of nylon across the hoop, but running in the opposite direction so that the two threads cross at the center, as shown. Thread the large tassel onto some nylon and hang this from the center of the hoop.

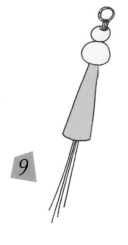

9 Cut four lengths of nylon measuring 14 in. (35 cm). Tie them to the bottom of the small metal ring and thread all four through beads for about 3 in. (8 cm). Use big beads if you can find them.

10 Now thread each of the four lengths of nylon with beads, using the same number of beads for each strand. Approximately 9½ in. (24 cm) from the end, secure each length with a piece of masking tape, just while you complete all four.

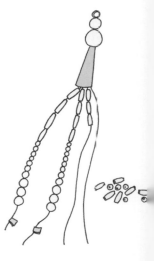

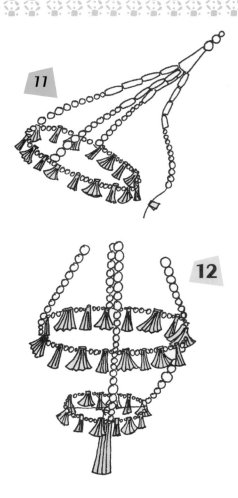

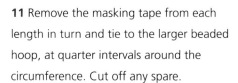

11 Remove the masking tape from each length in turn and tie to the larger beaded hoop, at quarter intervals around the circumference. Cut off any spare.

12 Repeat Steps 10 and 11 to make four shorter strands of beads measuring 4 in. (10 cm), with extra at each end for tying, and attach each one to the larger beaded hoop at one end and the small beaded hoop at the other.

13 Attach a length of nylon thread to the top of the metal ring, for hanging.

COLOR BLAST

Pops of Color

This mobile is simple to create and makes a stunning and stylish addition to any child's bedroom. Felt balls are easily obtained from craft suppliers and come in such a wonderful range of rainbow colors, they are hard to resist!

YOU WILL NEED

- Felt balls in different sizes and colors
- Needle and embroidery floss (thread) in different colors
- Scissors
- Length of ¼-in. (5-mm) doweling measuring 17 in. (43 cm)
- String

1 For this project, I used 28 felt balls measuring 1⅓ in. (3.5 cm) and 25 measuring ¾ in. (2 cm).

2 Use the needle with a length of embroidery floss (thread) measuring 34 in. (85 cm) to add the felt balls, varying the sizes and placing them 4 in. (10 cm) apart.

3 Place between nine and twelve balls on one length of floss (thread). Tie the two ends of the floss (thread) together to form a loop of strung balls.

4 Repeat Steps 2 and 3 to make six loops using a different color embroidery floss (thread) for each one. Vary the length slightly, too, so that each loop will hang at a slightly different height.

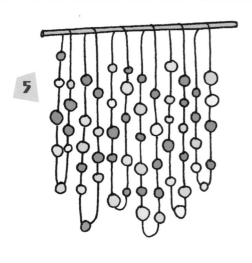

5

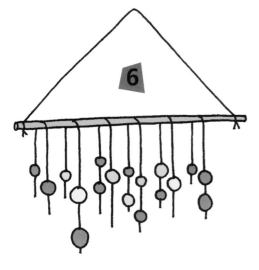

6

5 Hang the loops from the doweling, spacing them evenly along its length.

6 Cut a length of string measuring 24 in. (60 cm). Attach one end of the string to each end of the doweling, for hanging.

P<small>APER</small> C<small>ASCAde</small>

This mobile is so simple to make, yet makes a stunning focal point in a contemporary interior. It looks great hanging in a corner and you can change the lengths of the strands to suit its position. I chose a simple color palette and stayed with it, but you can go wild and use as many colors as you like!

YOU WILL NEED

- *3⅛-in. (8-cm) diameter circle template*
- *Colored paper (wallpaper and recycled gift wrap are fun to use)*
- *Scissors*
- *Twine or thick thread*
- *Craft glue*
- *Hoop (I used a 8-in. (20-cm) metal hoop from a craft supplier)*

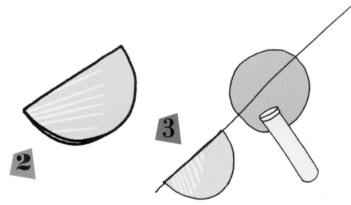

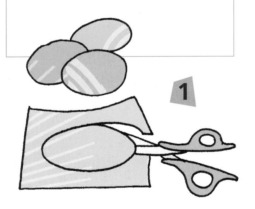

1 Use your template to draw lots of circles on different colored scraps of paper. Cut these out.

2 Fold each circle in half.

3 Take one length of twine measuring 35½ in. (90 cm), glue the back of a circle and stick the two halves together sandwiching the twine between them. Make sure the twine runs along the fold. Have some circles facing one way and some facing the other, for variety.

4 Make eight strands of semicircles and tie them to the metal hoop, spacing them evenly around its circumference.

5 Cut four lengths of twine measuring approximately 10 in. (25 cm) and attach to the hoop at the quarter points.

6 Gather the lengths together and tie the ends, making sure that the hoop is horizontal and the mobile hangs straight. Trim off any spare twine before hanging.

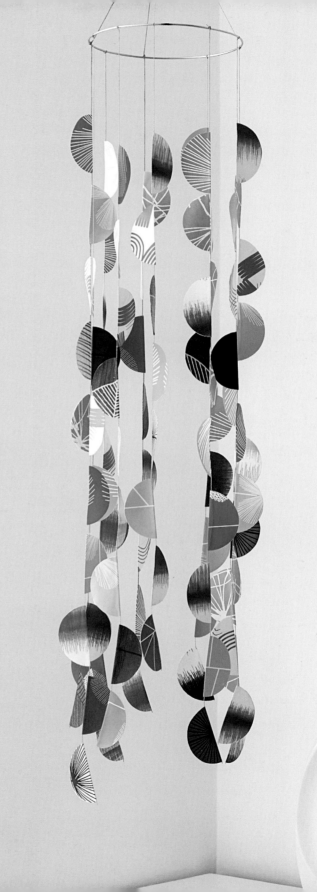

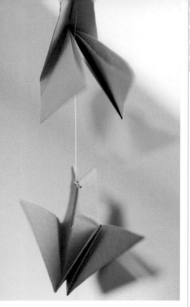

Origami Swans

One simple origami shape made in bright-colored paper and duplicated many times can make a stunning mobile. This looks fabulous in a child's bedroom—that's unless you want to keep it for yourself! I hung my origami from an embroidery hoop, but any hoop would work.

YOU WILL NEED

- *Thin paper in different colors*
- *Ruler*
- *Pencil*
- *Craft knife*
- *Cutting mat*
- *Needle and nylon thread*
- *Scissors*
- *Hoop*

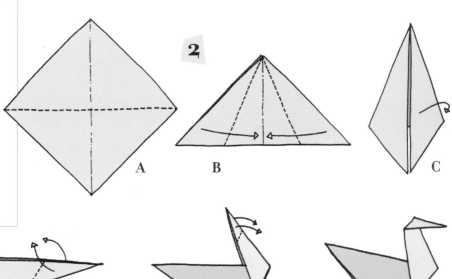

2

A   B   C

D   E   F

1 Cut the paper into a number of 3½-in. (9-cm) squares in different colors. Use a craft knife and protect your work surface with a cutting mat.

2 Follow the illustrations above to make each bird shape. I made 36 in total. Fold lines are drawn as dotted lines.

3 Divide the birds into five groups—vary the groups in both number and color.

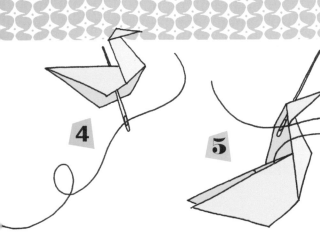

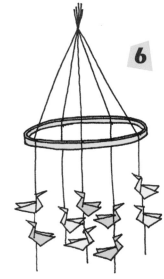

4 Thread a needle with nylon thread. Tie a knot at the end and begin to thread on the birds. Starting at the bottom of a column, push the needle up through the bottom of the first bird and out through the fold at its center. Position the thread toward the head end for a good balance.

5 Now take the needle up through the inside fold of the bird's neck and out through the top of the head, as shown. Thread all of the birds in the same way, leaving a 1–1½-in. (3–4-cm) gap between them. Leave 14 in. (35 cm) of spare thread at the top of each column.

6 Once you have made all five columns of birds, tie them on to the hoop. Space them evenly all the way around and leave plenty of spare thread for hanging. Gather up the five threads above the hoop and make sure that mobile balances straight, then tie a knot to join the threads together.

Tutti-frutti

These bright, fruity shapes will add a splash of color to a corner of the kitchen or in a kid's bedroom. Choose vibrant colors for the plain card stock (card) and some of your brightest patterns for the craft paper.

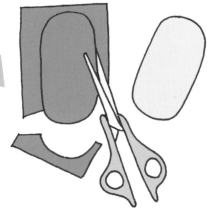

1

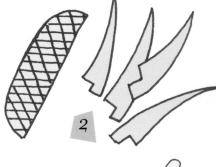

2

YOU WILL NEED

- *Templates, page 143*
- *Tracing paper*
- *Masking tape*
- *Pencil*
- *Thin card stock (card) in two bright colors for each fruit, plus some green for leaves*
- *Scissors*
- *Patterned craft paper*
- *Craft knife*
- *Cutting mat*
- *Craft glue*
- *Large sharp needle*
- *Nylon thread*
- *Wire cutters*
- *Florist's wire*
- *Small pliers*

1 To make a pineapple trace out the shapes from the templates and transfer the shape for the main part of the pineapple to each color of the card stock (card). Cut the two pieces out.

2 Transfer the shapes for the patterned section and the leaves to the patterned paper and green card stock (card) respectively and cut out the shapes.

3 Score down the center of each leaf shape. Use the very tip of a craft knife, making sure that the blade just breaks the surface of the card stock (card). Fold along the score line to make the leaf 3-D.

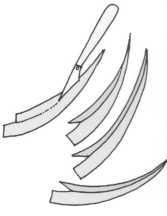

3

4 Follow the guide on the template to cut a row of triangles on one card stock (card) pineapple. Be sure to protect your work surface with a cutting mat. Just cut two sides of each triangle and bend the card back to create texture.

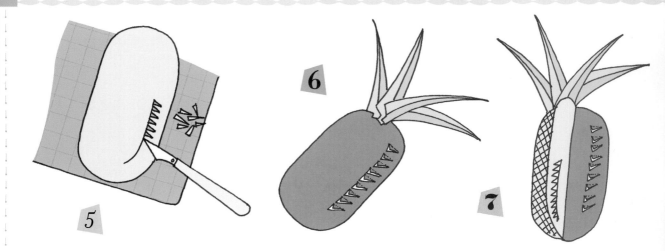

5 On the remaining card stock (card) pineapple, draw a pencil line ½ in. (15 mm) in from the edge, starting two-thirds from the top of the pineapple and following the curve at the bottom, as shown. Stop just short of the center point. Use the craft knife to cut out some triangles along this line.

6 Dab craft glue on the ends of the leaves and stick them to the top of the card stock (card) pineapple with the bent-back triangles. Position them to the left of the center point, but fan them out.

7 To assemble the pineapple, fold the second card stock (card) pineapple in half vertically and open out again. Glue the patterned pineapple section, face up, to the left of this vertical fold. Now spread glue on the back of the now patterned half of the pineapple and stick this to the first pineapple. Position it to the left, so that it covers the ends of the leaves. Use the photograph to the left as a guide.

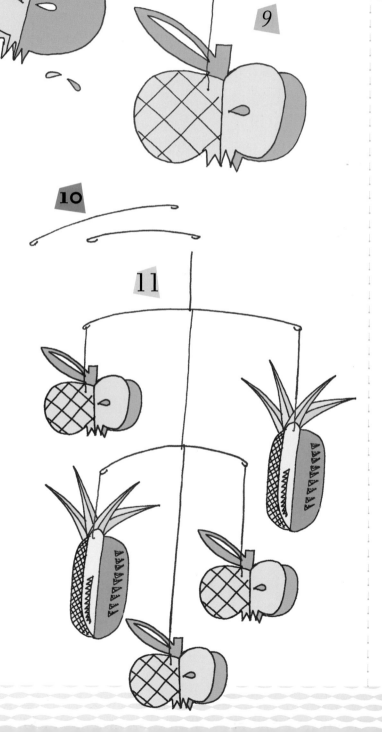

8

8 Follow Steps 1 to 7 to make another pineapple and two apples in the same way. Note that the two sections for the main part of the apple are not identical—use the version without the leaf as the second card stock (card) apple. Instead of cutting triangles, cut out pip shapes.

9 Following the guide on the template, use a large, sharp needle to make a hole in each of the fruit shapes. Thread some nylon thread through each hole and tie a knot to secure.

10 Cut two lengths of florist's wire—one measuring 11 in. (28 cm) and the other 8 in. (20 cm). Use pliers to bend a small loop at each end of the two wires.

11 Follow the illustration to assemble the mobile, attaching each fruit with a length of nylon thread. Finish off by attaching a length of nylon thread for hanging. When you hold the mobile up by this thread you can adjust the positions of the fruit threads to balance the mobile. You need a bit of patience for this. Once happy with the arrangement, dab some glue on the ends of the threads to secure them.

Paper-clip Graphics

The base for this mobile is so simple, it literally takes minutes to make. I have picked out cool-looking numbers from magazines for a contemporary graphic look. A series of black-and-white photos would work just as well, or use sections from your kids' drawings—cut and stuck on to card.

YOU WILL NEED

- *Florist's wire (see method)*
- *Small pliers*
- *Length of doweling measuring 13¾ in. (35 cm)*
- *Printed images*
- *Thin card stock (card)*
- *Craft glue*
- *Craft knife*
- *Ruler*
- *Cutting mat*
- *Paper clips*

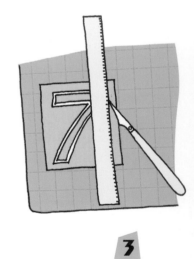

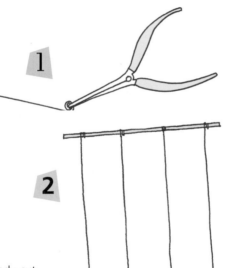

1 Use four lengths of ready-cut, straight florist's wire measuring 20½ in. (52 cm). Use pliers to bend just one end of each wire into a small spiral, and flatten.

2 Arrange the wires evenly along the length of doweling, winding the non-spiral end of each wire around the rod a few times.

3 If your images are printed on paper, stick them to some card stock (card) and trim them to the desired size. Mine are around 3 x 3 in. (8 x 8 cm). Use a craft knife and ruler, protecting your work surface with a cutting mat.

4 Insert one image into the spiral at the end of each wire. Use paper clips to attach the remaining images to the wires.

5 Bend a length of the florist's wire in half and attach it to either end of the doweling by winding it around the rod a few times, for hanging.

SWIMMING FISH

I have had this gorgeous Marimekko fabric for some time. I was waiting for the right project to come along and this fishy mobile seemed the obvious choice. The bold colors and graphic print work well with the simple lines of the fish shapes. I have used the same fabric throughout, taking different sections of the pattern for each fish. The mobile would also look lovely with each fish made from a different, brightly colored fabric.

YOU WILL NEED

- *Templates, page 140*
- *Tracing paper*
- *Pencil*
- *Scissors*
- *Medium-weight fusible interfacing measuring 24 x 24 in. (60 x 60 cm)*
- *Fabric measuring approximately 24 x 24 in. (60 x 60 cm)*
- *Iron*
- *Pins*
- *Needle and embroidery floss (thread)*

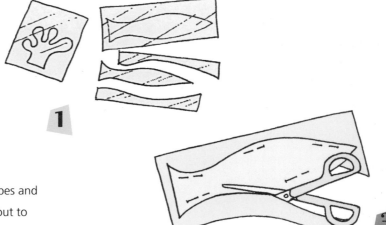

1 Trace the two fish shapes and seaweed and cut them out to make templates.

2 Follow the manufacturer's instructions to iron the fusible interfacing to the fabric. Fold the fabric in half with right sides together.

3 Pin the templates to the fabric and cut out the shapes. I made three large fishes, four small fishes, and one seaweed.

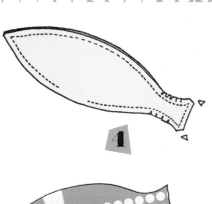

4

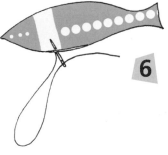

6

4 Pin the first pair of fish together with right sides facing. Sew around the edge taking a ¼-in. (6-mm) seam allowance and leaving a gap of 1 ¾ in. (4 cm), so that you can turn the fish the right way out. Repeat with all of the shapes for the mobile.

5 Trim the corners of each fishtail and snip into the curved seams of each tail and the curves of the seaweed. Be sure not to cut into the stitches.

6 Turn the pieces the right way out, press, and sew up the gap with small stitches. Make up the seaweed in the same way.

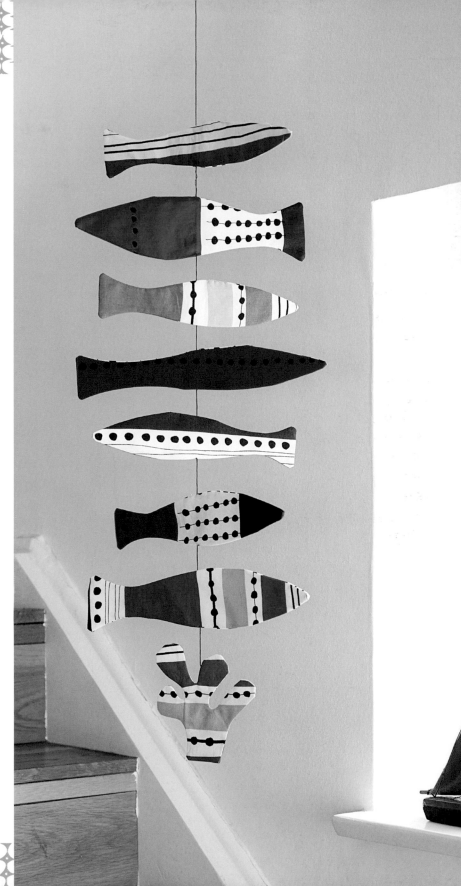

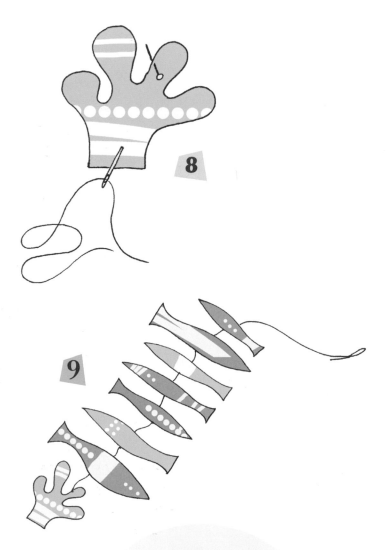

7 Arrange the fish in a column. Alternate the sizes and place them facing in opposite directions. The seaweed piece goes at the bottom.

8 Thread the needle with a length of embroidery floss (thread) measuring 32 in. (80 cm). Starting with the seaweed, push the needle in at the bottom of the shape and up between the two layers to emerge at the point of balance (see Tip). Pull the floss (thread) through, losing the unknotted end within the shape and securing with a couple of stitches.

9 Repeat Step 8 to attach the fish to the length of floss (thread), leaving 1 to 1½ in. (3 to 4 cm) floss (thread) between each one and securing each with a stitch to the top seam. Leave the desired length of floss (thread) emerging from the top fish, tying a loop at the end from which to hang the mobile.

Tip

To find the point of balance in each piece, pierce the top edge with a pin—at a point that looks central—and hold on to the pin while letting go of the piece. If the shape does not hang straight, move the pin slightly to the right or left until it balances correctly.

Pretty Petals

I have used a selection of gorgeous Japanese papers to make this delicate mobile of cascading flowers.

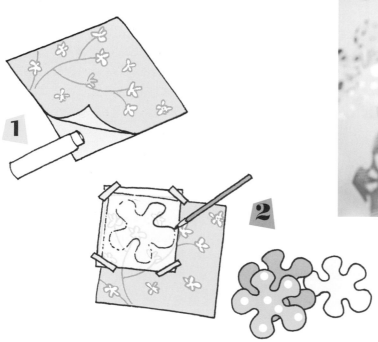

1 Glue a number of origami squares together, back to back. I like to combine a pretty floral print with a geometric pattern.

2 Trace out the flower shapes and transfer on to the origami squares. Use scissors to cut out the shapes. I made 25 flowers in a mix of the two sizes.

YOU WILL NEED

- *Craft glue*
- *Patterned origami squares*
- *Templates, page 140*
- *Tracing paper*
- *Masking tape*
- *Pencil*
- *Scissors*
- *Cutting mat*
- *Craft knife*
- *Thin card stock (card)*
- *Needle and cotton thread*

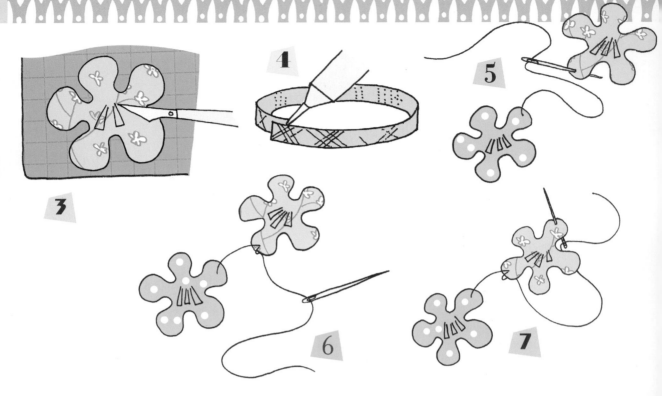

3 Protecting your work surface with a cutting mat, use a craft knife to make a few slits in the center of each flower. Follow the guide on the template, but cut them freehand—they don't have to be identical on each flower.

4 Cut a strip of card stock (card) measuring 14 x ⅔ in. (35 x 1.6 cm) and cover on both sides with origami paper. Bend the card to make a ring, overlap the two ends, and glue in position.

5 Divide the origami flowers into four groups, mixing up the sizes. The groups do not have to be equal. Thread a needle with some cotton and tie a knot in the end. Taking the first flower from a group, thread the needle from the back to the front, close to the edge of one of the petals.

Take the next flower and thread the needle from the front to the back, again toward the edge of one of the petals. Leave a ¾–1 in. (2–3-cm) gap between the two flowers.

6 Still working on the second flower, bring the needle round to the front and push it through the hole you just made. This will secure the flower in position.

7 Now take the thread across the back of the second flower to bring it up through the opposite petal. Thread on a third flower, from front to back, and continue in the same way until you have attached all of the flowers in this group. Leave 10 in. (25 cm) of spare thread at the top.

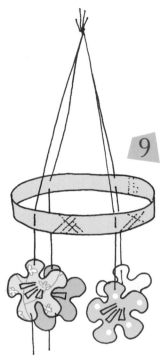

8 Make up the remaining three groups of flowers in the same way, varying their lengths. With the final column still threaded on to the needle, push the needle through the card stock (card) ring from the back to the front and back again, to make a large stitch in the card stock (card).

9 Attach the remaining three columns of flowers to the card stock (card) ring in the same way, placing them at quarter positions on the ring. Pull all the threads together, hold the mobile up, and tie a knot in the threads once you have the mobile hanging straight.

MATERIALS

To make some of the balancing mobiles you will need wire. It should be thin enough to manipulate using pliers, but not so thin that it bends under the weight of the decorative elements. I use florist's wire. It is a fine grade and comes in packs of ready-cut lengths. You will need some wire cutters and a small pair of bullnose pliers.

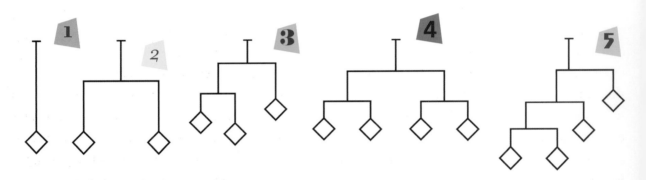

To construct a balancing mobile the main principle is that all the parts should be able to move freely without touching each other. Figures 1 to 5 show different configurations. When making a mobile with different levels, always start at the lowest element and work upward. Often, you need to hang the mobile in order to work on the balance. I find it useful to suspend the mobile from a doorframe using masking tape or similar.

I use hoops in many of my mobiles. You can buy small metal and wooden hoops from craft suppliers. Use them as they are or cover them with fabric or paper. Look out for old embroidery hoops in thrift stores. Lengths of doweling are useful, too, as are squared-off, thin strips of balsa wood. Both are available from craft suppliers. Alternatively, gather sticks from the garden that can be cut down to the required length.

I find nylon thread an essential material. It is strong and practically invisible. You can buy this from beading and jewelry suppliers. I also use thin florist's wire to join some of the hanging elements. This is sold coiled, in small amounts, and in a variety of colors. You could also use strong sewing thread.

A small hook screwed into the ceiling is ideal to hang the mobile from. Take care never to hang a mobile directly over a cot. Should it fall into the cot it could be harmful. Always hang it to one side.

TECHNIQUES

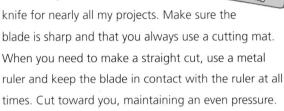

Adhesives

I use different types of glue for different projects, as well as a selection of adhesive tapes. When using glue sticks, try to find one with clear glue because this type never seems to clog up. Wood (PVA) glue is white when it goes

on but dries clear and is a very good adhesive for large areas. Use a brush or a small piece of card stock (card) to apply it. Strong, quick-drying glue is clear and usually comes in a tube. You will also need several types of adhesive tape, for instance: masking tape, double-sided tape, and clear tape.

Tracing

For many projects you need to transfer the template onto paper or card stock (card), using tracing paper. Place a sheet of tracing paper over

the template and secure with some masking tape. Trace the lines with a hard 4 (2H) pencil, then turn the tracing paper over and go over the lines again on the reverse with a softer pencil, such as a 2 (HB). Now turn the tracing paper over again and place it in position on your chosen paper or card stock (card). Go over all the lines carefully with the 4 (2H) pencil, and then remove the tracing paper. This will give you a nice, clear outline.

Cutting

I use a scalpel or a craft knife for nearly all my projects. Make sure the blade is sharp and that you always use a cutting mat. When you need to make a straight cut, use a metal ruler and keep the blade in contact with the ruler at all times. Cut toward you, maintaining an even pressure.

Scoring

It is important to score your paper or card stock (card) before making any fold. If it helps, you can draw a pencil line first to help you score in the right place. Place a metal ruler along the line and then score down the line, using the back (blunt) edge of a craft knife or the blunt side of a cutlery knife. Make sure you keep the side of the blade in contact with the ruler.

Backstitch

Bring the needle through the fabric and take a short backward stitch on the stitching line. Bring the needle through a stitch length in front of the first stitch. Take the needle down where it first came through and repeat to sew the seam.

Whipped backstitch

Work a line of backstitches (see above). Using a blunt needle, slide the needle under the thread of the first backstitch from top to bottom and pull the thread through. Repeat in each stitch in the row.

TEMPLATES

Most of these templates first need to be enlarged on a photocopier; all the enlargement ratios are detailed next to each template. Follow the instructions on page 137 to transfer the template onto paper.

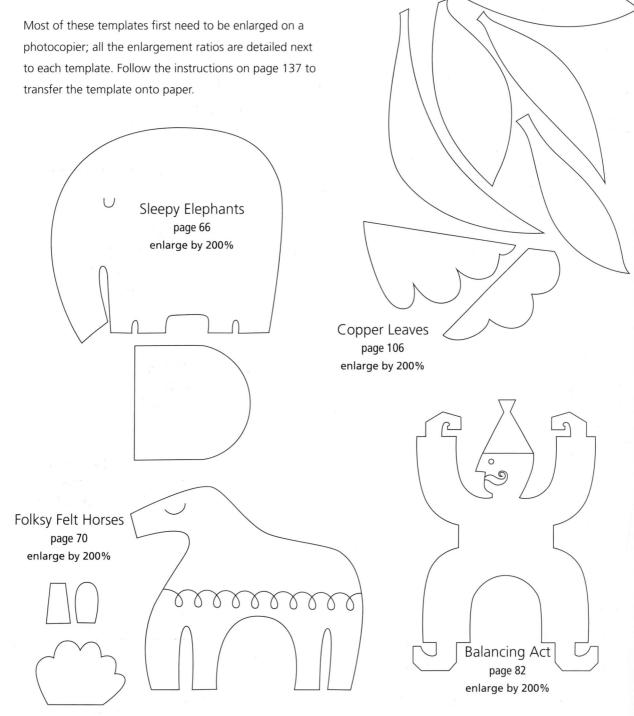

Sleepy Elephants
page 66
enlarge by 200%

Copper Leaves
page 106
enlarge by 200%

Folksy Felt Horses
page 70
enlarge by 200%

Balancing Act
page 82
enlarge by 200%

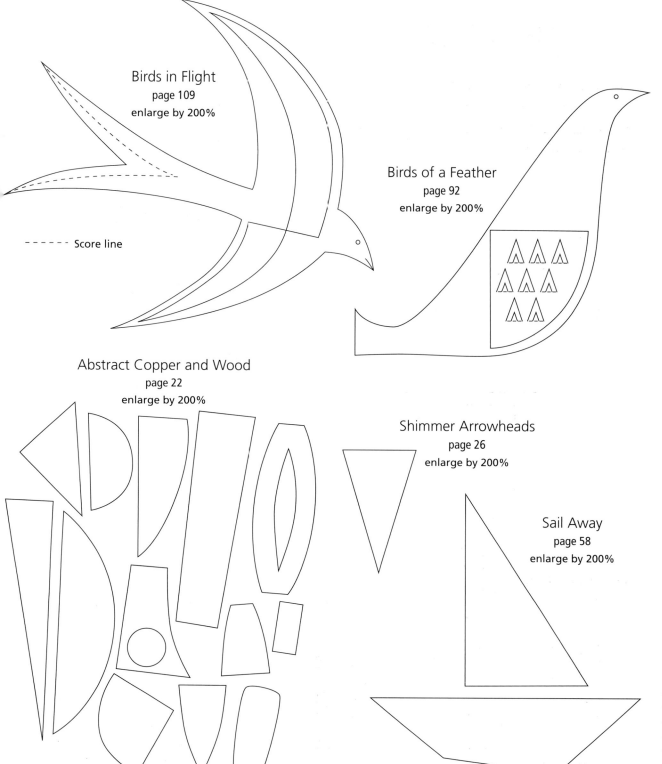

Birds in Flight
page 109
enlarge by 200%

- - - - - - Score line

Birds of a Feather
page 92
enlarge by 200%

Abstract Copper and Wood
page 22
enlarge by 200%

Shimmer Arrowheads
page 26
enlarge by 200%

Sail Away
page 58
enlarge by 200%

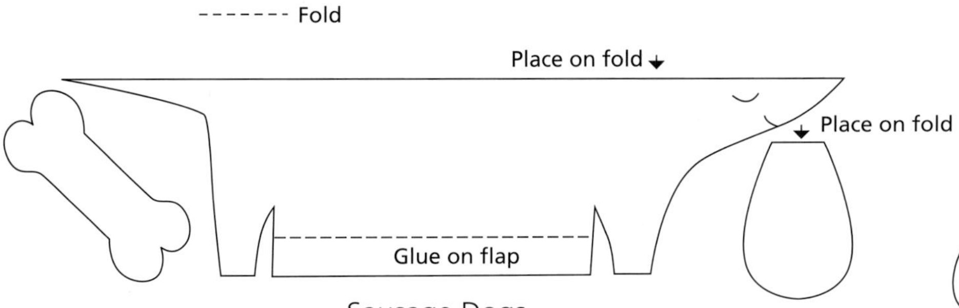

- - - - - - - Fold

Place on fold ↓

Place on fold ↓

Glue on flap

Sausage Dogs
page 74
enlarge by 200%

Pretty Petals
page 133
enlarge by 200%

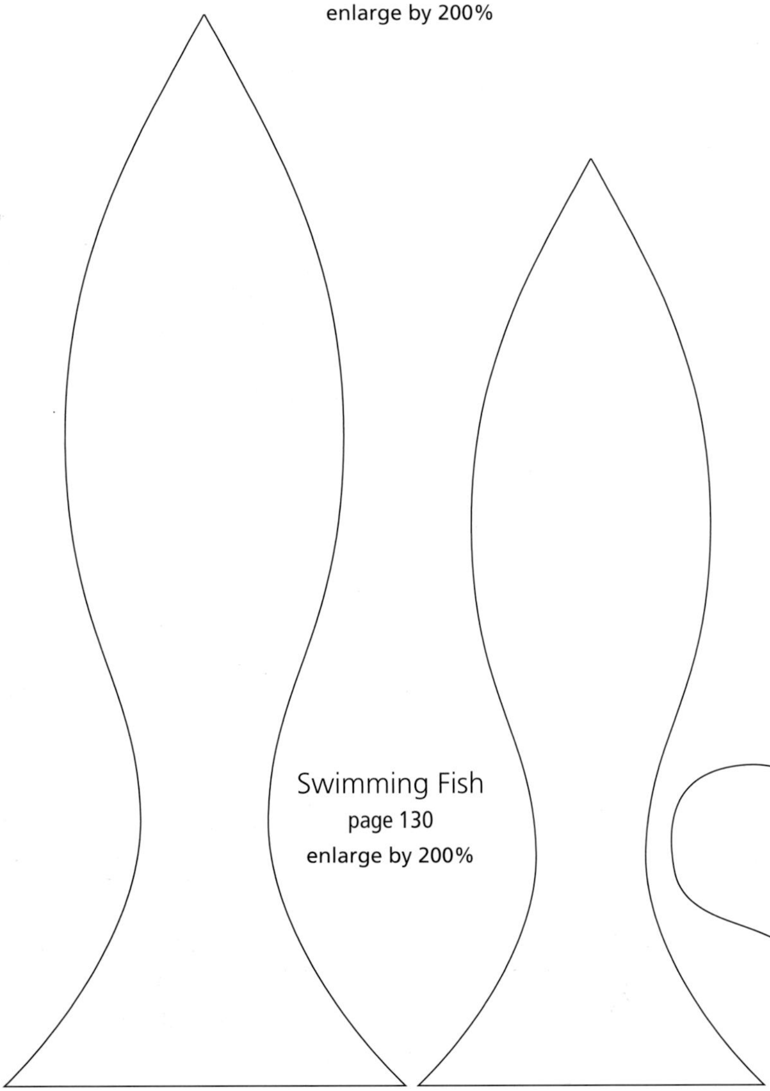

Swimming Fish
page 130
enlarge by 200%

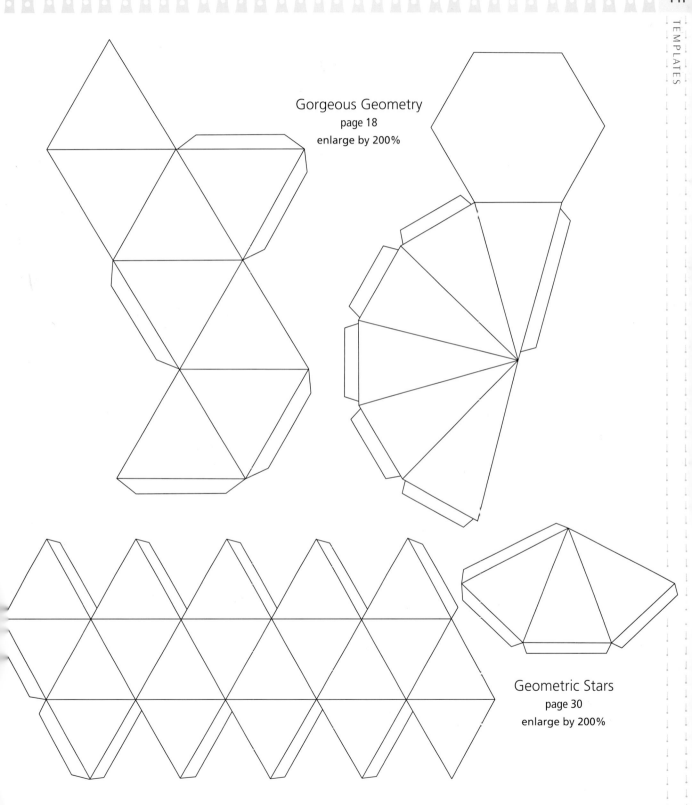

Gorgeous Geometry
page 18
enlarge by 200%

Geometric Stars
page 30
enlarge by 200%

Wild West
page 86
enlarge by 200%

Sky-bound Town
page 78
enlarge by 200%

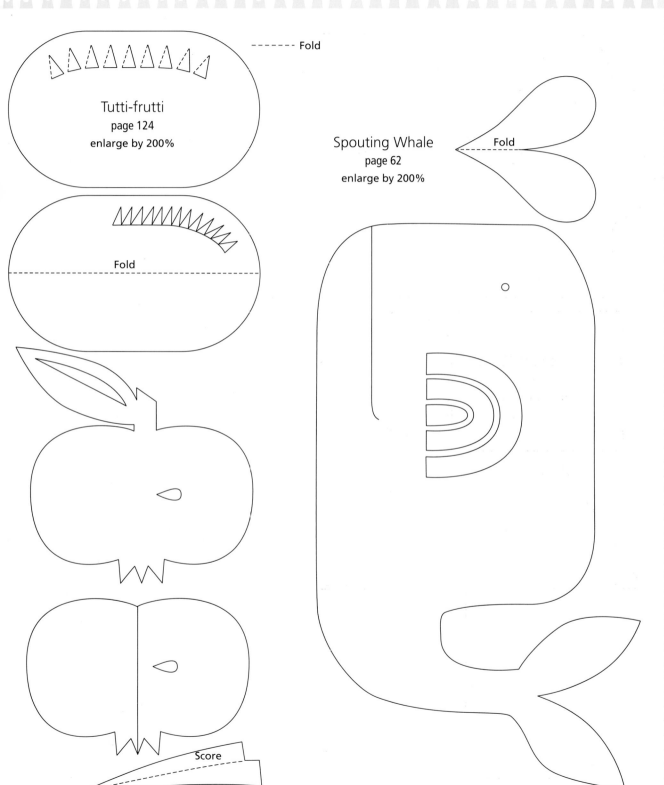

- - - - - - - Fold

Tutti-frutti
page 124
enlarge by 200%

Spouting Whale
page 62
enlarge by 200%

Fold

Fold

Score

SUPPLIERS, INDEX, AND ACKNOWLEDGMENTS

SUPPLIERS

US STOCKISTS

A.C. Moore Stores nationwide
1–888–226–6673
www.acmoore.com

Crafts, etc.
1–800–888–0321
www.craftsetc.com

Craft Site Directory
www.craftsdirectory.com

Hobby Lobby
www.hobbylobby.com

Jo-Ann Fabric and Craft Store
1–888–739–4120
www.joann.com

Michaels
1–800–642–4235
www.michaels.com

UK STOCKISTS

Cass Art
020 7354 2999
www.cassart.co.uk

Cloth House
020 7437 5155
www.clothhouse.com

Craft Creations
01992 781900
www.craftcreations.com

Crafty Devils
01271 326777
www.craftydevilspapercraft.co.uk

Fabric Rehab
www.fabricrehab.co.uk

Shepherds Papers
020 7233 9999
store.falkiners.com

Hobbycraft
01202 596100
www.hobbycraft.co.uk

Paperchase
Stores nationwide
www.paperchase.co.uk

The Papercraft Company
07812 575510
www.thepapercraftcompany.co.uk

INDEX

ACKNOWLEDGMENTS

Thank you to CICO for giving me the opportunity to work on this lovely project, especially Cindy, Sally, Anna, and Fahema who always make everything run smoothly and are such a pleasure to work with. Thank you James for the brilliant and inspiring photography and going that extra mile to get things just right. Thanks to Anna Southgate for her careful editing and to Elizabeth Healey for creating such a great look for the book. Thank you Virginia at roddyandginger.co.uk and Shelly and Sean at etcetera-online.co.uk for letting me shoot in their gorgeous homes and use their wonderful props. Thanks as always to my lovely family, Ian, Milly, Florence, Henrietta, and Harvey, who are always on hand for support, advice, encouragement, and untangling tangled mobiles!